MY LIFE
UNDERWATER

BOOK ONE

CHARLES E MARTIN

I've always written.

For as long as I can remember I've written. But I never really knew what to write about. If I had a dime for every book or piece I began writing but never finished, I'd be the wealthiest and least successful writer on the planet.

When I met Kitten, my Queen, my writing style began to change. But I still didn't know what to write. I won't explain here what happened.

I'll save that for book two.

One night, after a profoundly moving conversation between She and I, I woke up somewhere around two in the morning and I began writing. My mind was flooding with ideas and images and memories and all the right words to give real voice to those memories.

When the sun came up, I snapped out of my spell and slept for a few hours. But then I continued. And I didn't stop for several months. There were several hundred gallons of wine that fueled my steady push toward something I was so sure of and so frightened of. I just ended a sentence with a preposition.
So I've proven my worth.

I hope it reads like it was written.

MY LIFE UNDERWATER

Kitten said it right, "Blood is nothing. It's mostly water."

Everything bad happens in July.
I remember that summer well. My father was home
more. My mother finally came out of her room.

She asked where the vacuum was. She spoke with her
back to us because she was ashamed of her pain.

"It's not good for the kids! Don't you understand?
It's not good for them, you selfish prick!"

Then my father left us.
For nearly three weeks he was in the hospital, in a
small Idaho town we accidentally fell into. More than
a mile from home, he hid from us. So stoic and still,
in some hospital bed.

"How could he do this to us?"

My mother was furious.
It was only four weeks until school began.

Everyone seemed fine for the Fourth of July. Uncle Ronaldo and Aunt Lulu were wearing matching t-shirts from Wildwood, New Jersey.

Mom and Dad were shaking the sand off the blanket. Their friend, Bridgette was drinking wine from a bottle with a nun on the label. She was happy and looked like a younger and prettier version of mom.

I remember her like a Christmas ornament. A shiny, warm, and irregular lens flare in my childhood vision.

It wasn't just me who felt close to her. Mom and Dad fought about her so I knew Bridgette was important. They only fought about important things. Like money and whiskey. She meant something to all of us. She helped my sisters with their hair when mom was sick. She got me a sandwich and drove me to the scout meetings each Wednesday for quite a while.

Then my mother got a little better and came out of bed and wanted to give Bridgette a chance to do other things.

"I'm your wife, you son of a bitch! Your goddamned wife! And these are MY kids! Don't you take this from me!"

Dad woke me up Saturday morning early. He wanted me to help him in the yard. It was always windy in Idaho. It bothered me. It was 1973.

I was eight years old. I was a seventies kid. My hair was long. My Idaho hair was constantly swirling around my eyes and mouth. I wasn't an Idaho boy. Idaho boys belonged to a different time. Their hair was cut short. You could see the skin in their hair. They called me a girl. They called me a faggot.

They rode up and down the street on their bikes in a group of four or five with their sweaty scalps shining in the hot morning sun. Each time they passed, they watched me and my father while we cut the lawn and swept the walk. Mostly, they watched my Father.

He was tall and handsome and sinuous and protective and territorial. Everyone seemed cautious around him. They wouldn't call me names as long as he was near.

A couple of the boys would show off with a wheelie or a sideways skid. Their curiosity kept them returning up and down our street.

Dad put the mower back in its place in the far corner of the garage next to the stack of empty Pop-Shop bottles. I followed with the push-broom. Dad told me to grab the plastic trash bag full of clippings. I ran back to the end of the drive and took hold of it and began dragging it toward the garage where the trash can lived.

"Pick it up! You'll tear the bag!"

His voice was deep and commanding. The bag was too heavy. I continued dragging it across the cement.

"I said to pick it up! Now look what you've done!"

I looked back and saw a narrow trail of fresh, green clippings across the hot, white cement. I looked at Dad's face. I could not always distinguish anger from disappointment with him. I felt stupid. I didn't know what to do next. Dad grabbed at the smaller broom and dust pan and quickly swept up the trail. He pulled another trash bag from the box on the shelf in the garage and popped it open like a parachute.

"Want to go for a ride on the motorcycle?" He asked me like it was an apology for being sharp with me.

"Yeaaaa!" In hindsight, my youth felt emotionally strung together with little events like this one. The events seem now, like a few faded wooden clothespins hanging randomly spaced across a swaying clothes line. The memories are useless and only had purpose while they were being made.

I remember skateboarding on the drive and hearing my mother yelling.

"Goddamned wind! Now I have to wash everything over again!

Again...

Again."

I ran to the back yard. She was on her knees gathering laundry that had fallen from the line. A cigarette held gracefully between the fingers of her left hand, she was in a silk nightgown that, when standing, landed just above her knees. Her hair was black, curly, and not brushed. She made me think about a baby deer on ice. Or the witch when she was melting.

There are no surprises with my mother. There is nothing mysterious about her. If you stand in front of her for more than three minutes, you know her.

People often compare feelings to the gut. It's because feelings live inside your dark, fleshy and damp places. My mother wears emotions like an ill fitting dress. It's embarrassing.

I helped her pick up the few items that had fallen.

I stood facing her with a few dish towels in my hands, and I could smell the detergent and fresh summer air in them. My mother lifted her head and sat up on her heels. She had water colors running from her eyes to her jaw. She held some blue bath towels in her right arm. She lifted her left hand to her mouth and let the cigarette loosely dangle from her lips. She looked up at my face. Was she trying to recognize me?

She used her cigarette hand to wipe her wet face and put her hand on my shoulder to help herself up onto her bare feet.

"I'm your goddamned wife! And these are MY kids! Don't you take this from me! I won't let you, you prick!"

Dad put the helmet with the green swirls on my head and fastened the strap. He held the bike steady while I climbed up onto the back of the seat.

He gracefully swung his long leg up over the seat, sat in front of me and I immediately wrapped my arms around his waist. He pulled the kickstand back, and pushed us backwards out of the garage. Once he had oriented the bike to the road at the end of the drive he stood up, set his boot heel on the crank and stepped hard on it. The motor fired up and growled. It made me smile with excitement.

Even then, I knew it wasn't cool to show my excitement. But I couldn't help it. This was a clothespin moment.

My father throttled it. We shot out of the drive and into the street like a cannon. We passed the short-haired boys on their bikes and I felt stronger than them. I could see their envy. I looked back. They were still. They were watching us disappear with lush curiosity.

Dad handled the bike with ease. He leaned and dipped the heavy machine into corners and popped up out of turns like a seasoned pilot. I admired it. I imagined myself holding the grip and throttle in my hands. I would never be that strong. I couldn't imagine being the man my father was.

It was a small town. We had only lived there a short time. But I knew the streets well.

We always traveled in small and familiar circles. We turned onto Park street not far from the city swimming pool.

This was Bridgette's street.

Her house was the small yellow one on the right at the end before the cul-de-sac. Dad slowed for the dip in the drive and we pulled up under the carport. Dad switched the motor off. It was quiet but I could still feel the buzz of the engine in my legs.

I always waited for my father to tell me what to do. I was never very sure of how things were supposed to work.

He loosened the strap and pulled his helmet off. He bent his tall frame and looked into the small round mirror mounted to the handle bars. He ran his fingers through his long brown hair.

"I have to go inside for a minute. You stay here.
I won't be long."

I nodded and scooted forward on the seat and put my hands on the grips. "Can I hold the handle bars?"
"Yes," he said. "But don't turn the key on."

He gave my helmet a friendly tap on top like you would a counter top after you struck a deal at a pawn shop. He turned and rapped on the aluminum screen door to the house. Not waiting for an answer, he opened the screen door, turned the gold knob on the wooden door and disappeared into the house. The door shut quietly behind him. My father never waited for permission. He never waited to be told what to do. He always knew how things worked.

We were different, he and I.

It was hot out. The sun was just starting to sneak down over the roof of the carport. It reflected off the shiny cement. I could feel my hair getting wet under my helmet. Should I take it off? I looked in the small round mirror. Sweat was dripping down my head near my ears. Damp curls stuck to the side of my neck like cat's claw running up the east side of our garage. There was a shady spot under a walnut tree in Bridgette's back yard. I could see it from where I was sitting.

I could take this helmet off and go sit in the shade for a minute. But Dad said he'd only be a minute. How long had he been inside? Why did I have to stay on the bike? I understood when adults didn't want kids around. That was normal. I didn't want to be inside with them. I just wanted to be not quite as hot as I was and I was unsure whether taking off my helmet and going to sit in the shade would show disrespect to my father.

I ran my thumb across one of the buttons. I thought that could be the horn. I could accidentally press it.

I couldn't remember just how loud the horn was. Maybe it would be a bad idea. I fidgeted with the button, not wanting to be startled by the sound of the horn.

Nothing.

Then I pressed it with intent.

Nothing.

I pressed it as hard as I could and held it.

Nothing.

I was never quite sure how things worked. But I knew that some things needed more power to work. Did I need to turn the key on? Dad said not to turn the key. But I didn't want to start the bike and leave.
I wouldn't ever leave him.

"How could you do this to me! I AM YOUR WIFE! How could you do this to your own flesh and blood! You selfish prick!"

I turned the key. My heart jumped and raced when I saw a green light glow on one of the gauges. I sat still for a moment. The green light stayed on. Nothing else was happening. The engine wouldn't fire up unless I kicked the crank. Everything was fine. All systems were go. I set my thumb squarely over the button that blew the horn.

I took a deep breath and pressed it.

The carport was like a tunnel. The horn blared like Uncle Ronaldo's VW. I took my hands off the grips and turned the key back to off. I could still hear the sound of the horn pinging back and forth from the concrete to the carport ceiling to my ears and back to the concrete again.

I sat still for a moment. I thought I heard the gold knob rattle on the door. I watched for it to open. I scratched the cat's claw from my neck and adjusted my helmet with both hands.

The knob turned and the door opened. My father swung the screen door wide open. He was so tall, his head nearly grazed the two-by-six beams of the carport roof.

It took two steps for him to reach me. He took me by the arm and ripped me from the motorcycle seat. I never understood how I was supposed to respond to my father's physical discipline. I fell to the hot concrete. My knees cracked and I caught my balance with one hand near my father's black leather boot.

Should I stand up? Should I compose myself? Should I allow him to orchestrate the confrontation? Was this a confrontation?

He grabbed me by the back of my shirt collar like a lion grabs a cub. I could feel the fabric burning the sides of my neck near my sweaty cat's claw. He set me on my feet. I thought I had my balance. I heard the crash of his hand across the side of my helmet. My feet were swept from under me and I hit the concrete head first and slid just a little bit. Only enough to leave a raspberry on my elbow and the side of my knee.

Should I stand up? Should I lie there and wait for him to arrange things the way he wanted? I sat up. My head felt heavy. Dad said it was an adult helmet but that it would work just fine for me.

He planted his boot next to me, bent down and grabbed me by the back of the helmet and lifted me up. He lifted me much higher than my actual height.

He probably didn't know how small I still was. I could never imagine being the man my father was.

I could feel the leather strap under my jaw. I couldn't breathe, but it was only for a minute. He dropped me on to the motorcycle seat. During this dance that me and my father did... This dance wherein he lead and I followed... A dance we often did... he was quietly yelling at me. I could never remember much of what he said. I suppose I was too busy remembering the steps.

He turned the key and cranked the engine and we raced angrily through the streets. I held on to his waist.

I didn't know if he wanted me to. But I didn't know what else to do with my arms. I was always told to hang on.

July was almost over.

I spent the last hot days of the Lion climbing the Elm tree in the back yard and writing angry messages in chalk to Paris--my older sister, out on the sidewalk in front of the house.

"I hate you"
"Your a fairy"
"Your a stuped and a fat pig"

I hadn't seen mom in days. Her bedroom door was always closed when I came upstairs in the morning. I was often told not to bother her. Dad was usually gone by the time I woke.

I don't know exactly what he did for work then. I know he had a lot of friends. Mom and Dad sometimes fought about his friends. I think she wished she had as many friends as Dad did. They'd often come to the house after they finished their work early in the evening and have drinks in the front room with my father.

Our front room was mostly furnished with antique furniture. Not the kitschy stuff you see in little shops in New England. It was old Italian furniture. Heavy enough that it took three strong men to bring our old ice box into the house summer before last. It had come over with my great grandmother from Europe. Now it sat in the corner of our living room and held all of my father's liquor and special glasses.

So often did my father's friends come around that I began to see them as an extension of my father. There were frequently three or four of them in the living room with my father. They weren't merely conoscenti. They were a tightly knit group of men. All of them resembled my father: handsome, tall, charismatic. Like my father, they always knew what to do next. They always seemed to know how things worked.

The other Idaho fathers in the neighborhood would occasionally congregate with their friends. But it was different for them. I would see them in their garages or in their driveways leaning against a car with cans of Olympia beer in their hands. And it was usually only one or two Idaho friends. It seemed to me that maybe they weren't allowed to meet inside their houses.

They were shorter men. They wore jeans and T-shirts and seemed dull. I would see their mouths moving as I rode past on my skateboard, but I could never hear words or laughter or the clink of glasses or cursing.

I stood shyly, in the hall. I leaned with my hands behind my back against the wall watching my father and the other members of his club.

Benny sat on the love seat. The cushions were ivory colored and it was framed with cherry wood that scrolled in dark shiny swirls at the front of the rolled arms. My sisters and I weren't allowed to sit there. It was only for some adults.

Benny was always in a dark suit and tie. His hair was slicked back with hair oil that I could always smell when I was near him. It reminded me of the smell of my grandfathers aftershave.

Mom didn't like many of my father's friends. But she liked Benny. My father didn't have any brothers but Benny looked like he could be my uncle. He sat comfortably in the corner of the love seat with his one leg slung over the other, bent at the knee. His foot dangling and bouncing when he laughed his loud laugh.

I always smiled when he laughed. Everybody did. You couldn't help it. Even if you didn't know what he was talking about or laughing about you still had to smile. It was impossible not to.

His right elbow rested on the arm of the love seat while he held his glass of brown liquor and ice just off of the ivory fabric. The same hand held a burning cigarette between two fingers. No one sat next to him. It would seem unusual for another man to sit in that small space next to him.

On the large couch to the left, perpendicular to Benny were Ronaldo and Rick. Uncle Ronaldo was brother-in-law to my mother. He dressed like Benny and was the tallest and loudest man in any room. He called me Charlie and frequently teased me. He held a cigarette in his teeth while he spoke to the other men and he shook his glass of ice like a bell.

"Charlie! Charlie! Bring the Scotch from the ice chest, young man!" He said with a smile. I moved quickly to the box and pulled the silver latch on the right side. It was dark inside until I pushed the door all the way open. I surveyed the several bottles.

"The GREEN one, Charlie! The GREEN one." Uncle Ronaldo was instructing me.

I could smell malt and peat and sour and it made my mouth water. Not in the way it does when you're hungry, but in the way it does when you're feeling sick to your stomach.

I put my hand around the neck of a green bottle. I pulled it straight up as if to slide it carefully from between the others. I could hear glass sliding against glass and I wanted to be cautious so I used my other hand to finish extracting the bottle from among its friends. I turned to show it to Uncle Ronaldo and waited for his approval. He would probably say something to embarrass me.

"The OTHER green bottle, Charlie!"

The room filled with laughter.

"That's Whiskey! I'm drinking Scotch! You know the difference, don't you Charlie?"

I turned back and replaced the Whiskey. There was a green bottle in front and I found the word 'Scotch' on it. Of COURSE. How stupid could I be. That was what my uncle always drank. Why would it be buried among the picked bones of the liquor pile. Of COURSE it would be in front. I could pull this one out with one hand and so I damned well did.

I turned and looked at my uncle for approval. He pointed his finger at me like I was a bull's-eye.

"That's the one! Now bring it on over and let's put it to good use!"

I carried it like a trophy with both hands in front of me and handed it to my Uncle. He set his glass on the old coffee table in front of him, unscrewed the lid from the bottle, and filled his glass halfway.

Why did they never fill their glass? Why did they only fill it halfway and continue to ask me to fetch the bottle for them? Were they mocking me?

Was it good manners like when we went to my grandmothers house for dinner and my father told me not to fill my plate with potatoes, but to just have a spoonful and if I wanted seconds I could have seconds?

Rick sat next to my uncle on the large sofa. Among Idaho Dads, Rick wouldn't be considered quiet. Among my father's friends he was the quietest. He still possessed the same flamboyance and confidence as the others in the club. But he never teased me or my sisters. He was always kind and polite with us.

He always drank his liquor more slowly than the others. He never asked me to fetch the bottle for him. He would always get up during a story that he would be telling and take a couple of steps toward the icebox, stop and turn to the other men and continue with his story until laughter erupted and then he would turn and continue toward the icebox where he would choose a bottle, pour a splash or two in his glass, return it to the icebox, close the door and settle back into his usual place on the sofa.

My father had difficulty sitting still. If he wasn't standing facing the other men in the room, he was momentarily seated on the brown leather ottoman or the piano bench. He often paced a few short steps back and forth from the living room to the large open hallway where I leaned my back against the wall. When he did this he was always talking, laughing, telling a story.

On this particular evening, while Benny had the floor with one of his stories about a physical altercation he had with two men at work, Dad briskly passed me. He went down the hallway towards the end and into he and my mother's bedroom. I heard their voices. Calm, but petitioning. Coaxing. Kind. A few seconds later Dad emerged and walked quickly back toward me. As he passed he pinched at my nose like he often did when he was in good spirits.

The smell of my fathers hands--his rough skin--will always be a hallmark of valuable memories I have of my father. It may be one of the most comforting smells I can remember.

He returned to the piano bench. He reached into his white shirt pocket next to a skinny, dangling black tie that hung loosely around his neck and pulled out a box of Marlboros. He slickly flicked the box upward and a couple of cigarettes popped their heads out like baby birds from a nest. He lifted the box to his mouth and pulled one from the nest. He nodded at Ronaldo who tossed him a book of matches. Dad struck the match and lit his cigarette in one fluid motion just like that cowboy on the horse in the commercial.

The loud and jovial banter continued. The smell of liquor filled the air. Smoke hung in the room.

The warm evening melted through the living room window and I could see the layers drifting in the sunlight like autumn chimney smoke dancing over rivers and trees. I was lost in the haze for a moment.

The smell of my father's hands still smothered me in a most wonderful way. It made me long for permanence. It made me hope for something softer and grander than all of the sharp little edges I had been rubbing against for so long.

I heard a door open. I looked down the hall to my left and saw my mother standing, staring at me. She was in a short summer dress with tall wedges and her hair was neatly brushed. I could smell fresh perfume. I was familiar with that forced smile. She looked back at the door and quietly pulled it shut. She walked toward me with her usual doe-like eyes and slightly unsteady, feminine gait. As she passed me she kept the uniform smile fixed but didn't stop at me. Instead she walked right out onto stage and began her performance.

She stopped at my father and bent down to kiss him. He removed the cigarette from his mouth and obliged with a short, genuine kiss. The other men stood up. She hugged my uncle first.

"You smell like sweat and Scotch," she said.

"Good Scotch though," he replied.

She gave Rick a hug and asked him how Bridgette was. Rick replied that she was "...Never home. You know Bridgette."

Then she gave Benny a big hug with quick, awkward pats on his back up behind his shoulders. Everyone sat down, except for my father, who walked over to the icebox--mom called it the 'medicine cabinet' where he retrieved a bottle of clear liquor and clean glass.

My parents were very particular about glasses. My father and his friends preferred the heavy thick glasses. They had large hands and held the glasses with a sort of masculine purpose. My mother and the occasional women that came to visit used the beautiful crystal glasses. They weren't that much smaller. But they seemed more fit for feminine hands.

Dad walked over to the love seat where mom sat next to Benny and set the delicate glass in her hand. He twisted the lid off the clear bottle and poured a bit more than a half a glass for my mother. Even in the heat of the summer, she didn't like ice. She wasn't like the other ladies who mixed their liquor with soda pop or juice or other things. She was simple in that way.
I always thought men appreciated her for that.

I heard the sound of kids playing through the front screen door just beyond the medicine cabinet. I walked over to my father, who was now sitting back on the piano bench and waited for him to finish talking. He turned his head to me and I asked him if I could go outside and play.

"Go outside, Charlie! Get out there and ride that skateboard! Show the other boys how it's done!" My uncle shouted.

Permission or a command from my uncle was as good as that from my father. I feared and respected my uncle in the same way I did my father.

I turned and dashed out the front door, barely slowing enough to push the short, metal latch. I stood on the porch staring out at the street where a few of the neighborhood kids were collected. Some were on bikes, a couple of boys were on skateboards. There were five or six of them and they all moved together like starlings in a tiny, earthbound murmuration.

At first, I thought I would go down to the street and mix myself with the purling. The stoop held me.

Behind me, through the screen I could hear voices and banter. My mother with her tinkling bell voice and the heavy and happy laughter of men who knew how things worked.

The cement warmed my bare feet. July held the sun just a little bit longer in her evening arms.

It was one of those nights that you remember forty years later. A clothespin moment. It lasts in your mind like film. Wearing and yellowing and taking on a grainy and golden quality. Some of the images bedim or lose their sharpness. But the moment is stamped on your skin.

It's why we wrinkle and scar and why we are in a soft and melodic decay. It's why we itch and scratch and blister and burn. Because we are little more than a fleshy collage of memories.

The light coming from the large front room window made the tall shrubs against the house look like large, green lanterns.

The streets were empty. The Idaho parents had called all of their kids in for the night. There was now more light in the house than in the evening sky.

It was never windy at night. Maybe mom should hang the clothes to dry at night. She probably wouldn't want to right now. She was busy with friends. I knew how important it was for her to have friends.

"Why is it always about YOU! You think all of this is for YOU, well what about ME! When is it MY turn! You are so damned selfish. You don't give a damn about me!"

I turned to the screen door. I reached for the aluminum handle, pressed the square button with my thumb, and pulled the flimsy door open. I put my fingers to my nose. They smelled the same way after I held pennies. The large spring above the door pulled it shut.

As I entered the living room, I heard music and quiet chatter. The stereo was on. There was a record on.
I could hear Band Of Gold by Freda Payne playing.
I passed the medicine cabinet and looked to the right.

Mom was sitting in the love seat next to Benny. No one else was in the room. They had all moved to the kitchen. Benny had a glass and cigarette in one hand and the other rested on my mothers bare knee.

He was telling some story about a broken bottle at a bar and a woman with her shirt unbuttoned. Mom's empty glass was on the coffee table in front of them. She was laughing and her head would occasionally land on Benny's shoulder. When that happened, he put his cigarette to his mouth, drew in, looked up at the ceiling, held his lips like he might whistle and blew smoke into the air. His gush became one with the layers already dancing in the room. His head dropped and he noticed me.

"Charlie! What gives? Come here, buddy."

Benny was always kind to me. I never worried that he might lure me into a trap and tease or embarrass me.
I walked toward the love seat. Mom's head bobbed off his shoulder and she looked at me. She smiled. It wasn't forced. It was never forced when she was with friends like Benny and when she was in a summer dress and drinking and talking. She looked at me and smiled and returned her head to Benny's shoulder. He leaned carefully forward to talk to me. Mom was forced to sit up straight. She uncrossed her legs and reached for a pack of cigarettes on the coffee table.

Benny put his elbows on his knees. He switched his glass and cigarette to the other hand. I approached quite close to him. Benny didn't make me nervous.

He was genuine. In the pair of years I had known him he had only been good to me.

Mom was lighting her cigarette. The ashtray next to the box of cigarettes was the ashtray that I remembered most from my youth. It was a permanent fixture in our home. No matter where we lived, it was always there. It was full of lipstick-stained butts, spent matches and ash. Benny reached out and put his hand on my shoulder.

"Is it too dark out to play?"
I nodded.

"Do you want to go downstairs and play now?"
I shrugged.

"Can you do me a favor, Charlie? Can you go over to the ice box and bring your mother some drink?"

"Yessir," I responded.

Benny squeezed my neck and shoulder firmly. He had strong hands. But it didn't hurt. I knew he could hurt me if he wanted to. But he didn't.

He released his affectionate grip and I skipped across the room to the medicine cabinet. I returned with the bottle my mother liked and handed it toward her. Benny gently grabbed it from my hands before my mother could take it. He smiled and winked at me. My mother smiled and fidgeted with her hair while Benny filled her glass almost full.

He replaced the lid and handed it back to me.
I returned it to the cabinet right where it always went. I turned back around and my mother was already drinking from her fresh glass.

She took two large swallows and as she wiped her mouth with the back of her pale hand, Benny winked at me and said, "You're a good man, Charlie Brown."

I smiled and with a bit of blush in my skin I turned toward the kitchen. As I passed through the hallway and rounded the corner into the kitchen I heard feminine voices. Before I could even see, I knew Bridgette was there. She had an undeniably contagious laugh. She never laughed because she was supposed to. She only laughed because she couldn't contain it. I could smell my aunt Lulu before I could see her. I've come to realize everyone has an aunt who wore that same perfume. She too, had a loud and jovial disposition.

When I entered the kitchen, my aunt was sitting at the kitchen table in the chair closest to me. Uncle Ronaldo and Rick were sitting around the back of the table, against the kitchen windows. The windows had frilly drapes that weren't designed for privacy, hanging on either side of each window. They had big yellow daffodils on them.

Dad and Bridgette were standing, leaning against the counter in the corner, at right angles to each other. My aunt stood up and came over to greet me.

The kitchen was small. Only three or four more bodies could fit in it. She leaned over and hugged me in her usual way. It always left me feeling jarred. She was animated and full of life. She had a gleeful energy about her that filled a room. As I grew older I couldn't take her seriously. When she stopped laughing and hugging and holding hands and kissing and pinching cheeks and ears and tussling hairs she slipped quietly into folded arms and empty, black eyes and hand wringing.

I wasn't sure what to do with her. By the time I had played my emotional card, she had shuffled and moved on to the next hand.

The men at the table continued their talking and smoking. Dad and Bridgette both looked at me and smiled. Bridgette's smile was warm and pretty. Dad's was slight, tight-lipped. Almost apologetic.

Dad had a lot of friends. Mom didn't have that many. The only ones she DID have belonged to my father. Bridgette was mostly Dad's friend. I don't think Dad ever minded that Mom and Bridgette became friends. I just think when they were all three together, my Dad was the first friend and Mom was the second friend. I think that's how it worked for them.

Bridgette stood like oil on canvas in her Biba dress that looked like she had plucked it from the deepest recesses of Banagher Glen in Ireland. She reached out toward me with one hand. She had elegant hands. They had a velvety voice of their own.

When she raised them for any reason it was like she was commanding the attention of the orchestra. The players all stopped everything they were doing. All their page turning and rustling and tuning and talking and even breathing. They would look into her hazel eyes.... and wait.... to be led.

Ahhhhhh. Antonio Janigro. Nocturne No. 20 in C-Sharp Minor. The cello carried me away.

Benny had put a new record on.
I could hear my mother crying from the front room.

"Bennnnnnnnyyy! Naaaaooooooo! No Bennyyyy!"

She sounded slightly annoyed and bordering desperation. I had seen my mother emotional. In fact, most of what I have ever seen from my mother has been raw, dirty emotion. Yes, dirty. Because when you are near it, you feel the need to wash afterwards. You feel coated in some irrational, gritty laminate.

Back then, I needed my grandmother or my father or someone who knew how things worked to wash it off for me.

Now I bathe myself.

My father breezed past Bridgette and me, bound for my mother. I followed him into the bawling.

"Bennyyyyyyyy. Whaaaayyyy youu changed this alwayssss change the MUSICCC!!! I LIKKKKED Payne and Herrrrr rrrrrringgg! Why do I NEVVERRR GET TO CHOOSSSSE?"

Mom was on her knees in front of the Zenith Diplomat. As if she were at the alter. On her knees while angels played. I felt Bridgette and the others come up behind me. I couldn't turn and look at them. I could only lock my eyes on the collapse that was my mother.

Dad was on one knee next to her. One of his large, lean hands cupped the back of her head while he looked into her eyes. He quickly glanced up at Benny, who was standing above them. Benny put his cigarette in his mouth, put both hands behind his neck like in the cop movies, opened his eyes like he needed to wake up and shook his head at my father.

Bach played and his strings cried and I felt the conductors hands raise.

Bridgette put her hands on my shoulders.

"Nooooooo! You donnnnn dooo thiss ta meee you sonnofabitccchhh! NOOOO!"

Why was she mad at my father again? He was trying to figure things out.

"Bridgetttttte!"

Mom turned my direction, but looked past me.

"Bridgetttte! Listen to me! Tell himm. Tell Benny.
Tell my husband."

She was talking quietly now.

"Tell my husband. Ring Of Gold. That's the song that I wannnnnnt na hear. Tell themmm Bridgettttte. Pleeeeezzzz. Please tellll them. FUCKKK! FUCK YOU!! FUCK ALL OF YOU! You have NO IDEA!"

She wasn't talking quietly anymore.

"YOU HAVE NO IDEA WHAT IT'S LIKE CARRYING ALL OF THIS!"

Mom stumbled to her feet, stepped toward me and fell at my feet. I could feel Bridgette gently moving me aside. She knelt with my mother and took her hands in her own.

"It's okay," Bridgette whispered with a smile, looking at her wilted face.

Mom sloppily turned her face to mine.

"Chuckkk. I lovvve you. You know. Youuuu knowww. I lovvvve you and that song that I knowww you like. Thatttts the right song. Right, Chuckk? Riiiiighttt?"

She grabbed my hand. It startled me. I flinched. Bridgette came between us. Dad put his hands on Mom's shoulders from behind her. He put his mouth near her ear.

I heard him whisper,
"Baby. It's ok. Sweetheart. Listen."

Benny had put on a new record.

"Baby, listen!"

Up to then, I'd never seen my father so soft and desperate looking. Bridgette sang with the record.

"I want to live.
I want to give.
I've been a miner
For a heart of gold.
It's these expressions
I never give
That keep searching
For a heart of gold.
And I'm getting old."

My mother stared into Bridgette's eyes so hard, I thought the two of them might burst. Bridgette helped her up. They put their arms around each other. They hugged and my mother cried softly. They danced, slow.

"I've been to Hollywood,
I've been to Redwood.
I crossed the ocean
for a heart of gold.
I've been in my mind,

It's such a fine line
That keeps me searching
for a heart of gold.
And I'm getting old.
Keeps me searching."

Clothespin moments. Strung out across the line.
Spinning in the dry wind.

When you reach up and pull them off the line and
look at them closely, you see them for how cheap and
small they are.

Water stained and barely held together by rusty springs.

This is where I landed.

When I plummeted from whatever pre-mortal reality
the gods carved me into, this was my landing place.

> This is all they had LEFT? NO ROOM
> AT THE FUCKING INN? REALLY?
> THIS IS MY GODDAMNED
> FUCKING BIRTHRIGHT? EVEN
> ESAU GOT A FUCKING BOWL OF
> LENTILS. WELL, WHERE THE FUCK
> are MY lentils? HUH??? WHERE ARE
> MY FUCKING LEGUMES?

The evening my mother had her vodka meltdown in the living room, once Benny and Uncle Ronaldo and Bridgette and Dad got her settled down and put away for the night, I lied in bed in my room at the foot of the stairs in the basement.

It was unfinished--this would become a pathetic metaphor for the rest of my life.

I had a twin bed on a metal frame positioned against bare two-by-four studs. Dad removed the insulation and said he would finish the walls for me before fall came.

A few feet across the bare concrete floor--Dad said he would put padding and carpet down when he got paid by one of his clients--was a four drawer dresser. There was a small lamp on it. Sometimes I tried to switch it off and see if I could stand the absolute darkness.

Usually I would just leave it on while I studied the wiring woven into the two-by-fours and drifted in and out of sleep. I traced the grain of the wood framing with my fingers and dismissed my discomfort over the contrast between my clean white sheets and the dull, raw wood that brushed against them. Such a small space with so much discord. My young, weak frame held between so much bare, pitted concrete. The sheets Bridgette had washed rubbing against splintering studs. My hopeless, little dresser lamp scratching for purpose in the dark, wettish margin of that moment. It was mine. It was where I would always be.

I could hear the sliding of feet above me in the kitchen. Chairs slid across the linoleum and sounded like broken trumpets. I heard muffled voices and laughter more tempered than earlier.

It was all quite comforting. They weren't the specific sounds that slowed my heart. It was the distance between me and the people I knew that warmed me. It was all of the sounds that run like water over rocks that pushed me headlong into a happy sleep. This was the water-colored static that filled the concrete spaces of my childhood.

I pulled the sheets back, sat up in bed, swung my feet onto the bare cement, and leaned over to the dresser. The cheap, little reading lamp was hot and smelled of plastic. I reached for the switch and turned it off.

I was happy Bridgette had washed my sheets.
I was happy my feet were getting warm. I was happy to hear that people were living and not sleeping in the rooms above me.

When I was six, my family lived in an apartment made of red brick and a black wrought iron rail along the front steps.

That was where I fell down the stairs on my bike and broke my first arm. I got mononucleosis that year. Some small town 1st grade teacher decided I was a genius. That was the year Nixon ended the US trade embargo with China. India and the Motherland became friends, and America was telling Vietnam to shave her legs and practice her lines for the next show.

My father packed up our family and we left the east coast for a simpler life in the west. My mother said we had the nicest unit in the duplex. The other unit was being rented to Mexican immigrants.

"They're dirty. All they do is look at your sisters and say dirty things about your mother. Lazy drunks."

Mom told us about the Mexicans. How they hated us and how they would eventually steal our homes and our mothers and sisters and our jobs and how we would have to leave our place and become nomads.

None of us had jobs except for my father. And he LIKED the Mexicans. If he wasn't scared, I wouldn't be either. I liked the Mexicans.

When they were out front loading up their strollers with sippy cups and diaper bags and sandwich bags full of dry Cheerios and getting ready to go shopping at Skaggs, I would climb the stairs and pretend to prepare my bike for a ride. I would sit on the seat and adjust my grips and kneel down and touch my oily chain and watch the mothers pack their little Mexican immigrant babies into their seats. It seemed strange to me that I couldn't understand what they were saying.

Maybe my mother was right. Maybe they were saying terrible things about her or my sisters. I was the bad one. Why wouldn't they say bad things about me? My sisters were always good.

One time while we were eating dinner at the kitchen table, my father suddenly reached across the table and slapped my sister, Paris across the face because he said he could hear her eating. She fell off her chair and began wailing. He demanded she stop or he would have to slap her again. She obeyed.

The Mexican mothers pushed their caravan onto the sidewalk. They smiled at me and said hi to me as they passed. How did I understand them! Maybe I had a special ability! Maybe my teacher was right! Maybe I was a genius! It sounded just like OUR language.

I could smell fresh laundry on their clothing as they passed. They seemed like nice people who were clean.

I never saw the fathers.

I think they must've been out looking for homes to steal.

That evening I was sitting on the curb watching cars pass and imagining what it would be like to drive each of them. I imagined how it would feel to position myself behind the steering wheels as I settled into the various styles of seats.

I was growing taller. It would feel good to look over the wheel at the road ahead. I would roll the window down and nod at the neighbors as I drove past them in their yards and their kids would look at me with jealous eyes. I would drive fast and the engine would roar. I would play a song on the radio and it would echo between the houses and through the neighborhood.

I wanted this, and with an appropriate amount of will, it would happen. Dad would sit in the passenger seat and counsel me. He would gently reach for the wheel with his long arm and make needed corrections as we cruised through the quiet city streets of our sleepy summer town.

He would smile at me and tell me what a good driver I had become. He might even pretend to fall asleep to prove his trust in me.

I sat on the curb and smiled.

I heard my father call to me from the back yard.
I jumped to my feet and ran thru the carport, grazing my fingers along Dad's Dodge Charger from bumper to breast bone, pushed through the wooden gate and burst into the back yard. He was standing next to a bike and examining it. He looked at me as if he wanted my approval.

"The old tenants must've left this. It's in good shape. Wanna take a ride?"

It was a dark blue Schwinn with a wide, blue and white seat with an 'S' on it. It had dirty, white handle-bar grips and grubby white wall tires.

"Both of us?" I asked.

"Yea! C'mon, son."

He pushed the bike through the gate and past the Dodge where he stopped and mounted the bike. I walked up next to him, studied the bike and waited for instructions.

"Come on."

He put his hand under my arm and pulled me up.

My legs scuffled about, trying to find a place among the bars and my father's legs. I was always so clumsy. I eventually determined that he was trying to land me on the handle bars, facing him. He got me in position with my butt in an uncomfortable spot centered on the handle bars. I held his shoulder with one hand and his forearm with the other. I shifted my butt so that there wasn't hard metal up in it.

Dad asked if I was comfortable.
"No," I whined.

He asked if I wanted to turn facing forward. It seemed like a more logical way to ride a bike, so I nodded.

He planted both feet on the concrete, stood up and place both hands under my arms and lifted and turned me around. I shifted and squirmed to find a less painful situation. I placed my bare feet on the front fender. If I put more pressure on my feet, I could lift my hips just enough to relieve some of the discomfort in my butt.

"Hold on, Son."

We rolled off the rounded driveway curb and it jarred my tailbone. I could feel Dad's breath on my back as he pushed the pedals and we gained speed. The road was smooth, the sky was filled with the soft parasol of Elm, Oak, and Linden. Suddenly, nothing else mattered.

I could feel the wind streaming between my dirty toes. I splashed my feet in the summer air like it was cool water. I closed my eyes and I felt my mouth smiling involuntarily. I could hear the air swirling around my face and hair.

The streets were empty. An occasional old man stood in his yard and watched us pass. A dog barked.
A crow cried.

Everything hard was slipping quickly past me and becoming smaller. My father's breath was heavy. It smelled like cigarettes and coffee. I could feel him smiling like I was.

We approached an intersection and a car was coming. My father reversed the pedals to brake. I was unprepared and I slipped off the handle bars.
There was no recovery from this.

Before my crotch hit the front fender my right foot got caught in the spokes of the wheel. We came to a bungling stop due to my leg being trapped between spoke and fork. The rest of me landed on the warm pavement.

I wasn't sure if I was truly hurt but it seemed awful.
I began howling.

My father was grappling with the bike and trying to get to me. I could see the frustration in his face. It was damp with sweat. Now I could smell oil and taste metal. I put my hand to my crying mouth and pulled back fingers webbed with saliva and blood.

Dad got a hold of me and worked at trying to get my bleeding leg out of the spokes. I was screaming mostly out of fear now.

The car that had caused our braking passed slowly and the family glared through their windows at my personal tragedy. A girl smaller than me pressed her nose against the inside of the back window and examined us. Her father rolled his window down.

"You okay?"

"Yes. Fine."
My father dismissed him like he did most men.

They continued down the road.
People were coming out of their front doors to see what the fuss was about.

"Is he okay? Do you need help?"
"Nooooo. No. We're fine! He's fine!"
My father was trying to remain calm.

"Son! You're fine. Stop crying! You're fine!" He was doing that quiet yelling thing through clenched teeth.

My face was wet with heat and tears and saliva. My leg was still stuck in the spokes. Was there more blood? It looked like it.

"Get up! You're fine! Come on! Get up!"

He rolled the bike forward enough to loosen the frame's grip on my calf. He pulled it from the spokes while I escalated my bellowing.

Before I knew it, I was up over my father's shoulder like a sack of potatoes while he pedaled the old Schwinn toward home. I squirmed until I slid down into his lap. He struggled to pump the bike so he kept lifting me upward with one arm.

I would never be the man my father was.

"Stop your crying! You're fine!" He whisper-yelled in my ear. His sweaty face slipped across mine.

People stopped and stared at our rolling catastrophe.

"Have these people nothing better to do?"
This time my father was actually whispering.

He didn't brake for the rounded driveway curb. He coasted to the rear bumper of the Dodge, dropped the bike on its side, stepped over the spinning front wheel, holding me high on his shoulder in one arm.

Mom burst through the door with panic spread across her face. She must've heard my cries.

"What happened!"

"He's fine!"

"Is he okay!"

"He's fine!"

"Is he bleeding!"

"He's fine!"

"Bring my baby here!"

Dad met mom on the stairs of our basement apartment. It felt like he was getting ready to toss me away.

"What the hell is wrong with you?"
He was whisper-yelling.

"Shut up, you fool! Do you have any idea how embarrassing you are?"

He handed me off to mom. He always knew what to do. My father knew how things worked. He never waited for someone to tell him what to do.

Mom held me in her arms the best she could. I was a soggy thrash-about. Convinced I was going to die in a basement apartment with thin walls and the immigrant family next door would know all the sordid and intimate details of my demise.

Mom took me to my bed. She calmed me and cleaned my wound while I winced at her every gentle touch.

Evening was filling my room with soft, blue light. Mom left me on my back, in my underwear with a cool wash cloth on my shin. She mumbled a weak little prayer in her bird-like voice then left me to rest.

She left the door ajar so that only a little light peeked in from the hallway. I hoped my father would forget about my foolishness. I hoped he would forgive me for embarrassing him.

My eyes were heavy. Only an occasional whimper was left from my bicycle tragedy.

Sleep. That's what I needed. Everything would be better tomorrow.

I felt a warm weight in my lungs that slowed my breath and buried my suffering.

Your Gods built us up like sand castles.
Glorious and fragile.
They stood in their paper boats,
and pushed out to sea.

Now they live below,
with all of your other treasures.
Pray to them.
They will wash us all away.

Water was rushing through the yard.

I ran through the kitchen to look out the window above the sink. The narrow pass between our house and the neighbors was filling with water rapidly.

Not like the clear, warm water my sister filled my tub with. This was cold and dirty and filled with debris.

I could feel the house shudder and groan. This was no flood. This was something cataclysmic.

My sister, Paris came running up the stairs from the basement, screaming.

Now I knew this was serious.

My mother must have been sleeping.

I could hear my father yelling at us from another room. "Stop yer screamin! It's no big deal!"

I ran from window to window surveying the situation. The streets were filled with rushing water. I could see water pouring into the neighbor's front door.
I felt the house begin to shift.

Noooo! What is happening?

Paris was yelling and flailing. I ran toward the kitchen. My bare feet hit the cool linoleum and I made eye contact with my sister. Her eyes were drenched in panic. We both stood perfectly still with our arms out like we were worried about our balance.

The sound of the water was deafening.

Suddenly, the house made a terrible noise and broke away from the foundation.

My sister and I screamed and fell into each other's arms. I could feel the house bobbing and swaying. My sister was only whimpering now. She held me so tightly, I could hardly breathe.

Was this it? Were we going to drown?

I closed my eyes and buried my face in her neck.
The house bucked hard and we were thrown against the cabinets. We cried and held each other in earnest.

I could feel cold water at my ankles now.

God.
No.
Not this way.
Not without my mother here to hold me.
Where was my father? He would know what to do.

I fell into a swirl of water and clouds and sleep and struggled to scream or open my eyes. When I came to, I was in my bed gasping for air. I opened my eyes and Paris was sitting on the edge of the bed at my feet and patting my ankles and legs with a cool, wet washcloth. She asked if I was ok.

"I had a bad, bad dream."

She gave me a hug and told me not to worry.
I looked around the room. No water. The apartment was intact. Everything was ok.

Paris is my older sister. We're close. Not geographically. But emotionally.

She is a year older than I. We were close growing up. In fact, she quite nearly raised me. During the years my mother was sleeping, if my father was busy, Paris entertained me, made me food, helped me with my clothing and homework. We played together as kids and shared mutual friends. We often slept in the same bed together until she was nearly twelve. During our teen years Paris was a good student and behaved in a way that made our parents proud. I was a terrible student and a rebellious kid. I was always in trouble.

In ninth grade, at the end of the school year when the weather warmed up, the drive-in theater in our small town was showing The Champ or Rocky II or Kramer vs. Kramer or something that wasn't rated R. I convinced my mother that I should be able to take the car with a friend. He would drive because he was a year older than I and he could legally drive at night.

Paris was there that night. It was her first date with the man she would eventually marry. He was tall, small town handsome, and jockish. He was prom king.

Every boy wanted to be him and every girl wanted to be with him. When he and Paris married two years later, he was offered a full ride basketball scholarship to Gonzaga university.

Paris was tall, beautiful and athletic. She was prom queen. Every girl wanted to be her and every boy wanted to be with her.

This is what I was up against. Prince Charles and fucking Lady Diana.

By the end of the night I was wandering from car to car over the sloping gravel hills of the drive-in, putting my slobbery, drunken, mouth on every windshield in the theater, looking for my sister. Think James Dean in A Street Car Named Desire.

I finally found her, appropriately cuddled up to Prince Charles in the front seat of his father's 1980 Nissan Maxima. Paris told me to go home. I did.

Quite a few hours later, I learned that she didn't rat me out to my parents. She had no interest in throwing me under the bus. My parents would never have known that I had been drinking had I not thrown up a case of cheap American beer and four drive-in hot dogs all over the floor of the only bathroom in our house, conveniently located in the hall next to my parent's room.

Paris and I were always close. I've always respected her.

Blood is mostly water. We bathe in water. We drink it. We wash our clothes and our cars with it. We clean our teeth with it. We flush our shit in it.

Blood means nothing until you've lost enough of it.

When your veins are dry and you're a shell, you become powerless. You've nothing to give. Soon you have no connection to anything living. Soon everyone stops asking you for anything.

Hope and Christina were my younger sisters. Hope was about eight years younger than I and Christina was right behind her.

When I survey the landscape of my past and more particularly, my youth, I can remember little to nothing of my younger sisters. Paris and I agreed that they seemed almost part of another family.

Our parents were different for them. By the time Hope and Christina became teenagers, Paris and I had married and started families of our own and our parents had all but checked out.

I'll always remember the way the chestnut tree in the backyard smelled.

Like black pepper and grass. That warm Saturday morning I sat in the grass with the Idaho wind tussling my hair and growing pains pinching my knees.

I rubbed the tree leaves between my fingers and put them to my nose. My fingers were sticky so I rubbed the sap on my jeans. I pulled handfuls of grass out of the ground because I was bored.

I could hear the bike gang playing in the street out front. Their squawking and carrying on washed up over the rooftop and poured down the other side into the backyard. I didn't care very much about them that day. It took too much work to protect myself from their mocking and jabbing.

Plus, Devon had a fresh crew cut given to him by his mother and she cut the top of his head so that he had a bloody little gash in his sweaty head now. I hated looking at it.

His mother was loud and drank beer from a can. She acted hard and always seemed angry. I don't know why she wouldn't just take Devon to the barber. I hated looking at that bloody fissure on his head.

It was much better just to sit in the backyard and throw grips of grass at the neighbor cat as he sat staring at me in attack position from a few feet away. He was small but he made me nervous.

I thought about Devon's grotesque head wound again.

A car pulled into the driveway. It was too early for it to be Dad. He wouldn't be home for another four or five hours. The tires screeched on the cement as the car broke hard. I got to my feet. My knees were stiff and sore. I dusted grass off my backside. My pants were damp from sitting in the shaded lawn.

When I got to the driveway I saw my Aunt's red Ford Country Squire station wagon parked there. It was ticking and hissing the way a car does when it's pushed hard and then parked.

I ran up the steps to the back door. I could hear crying and frantic expressions. I opened the door and stepped into the kitchen where my Aunt Lulu was standing with her face in her hands.

She heard me enter the room and her hands slid down her cheeks exposing her wet eyes. She looked at my face but through me.

"I'm hurrying! I'll meet you in the car!" My mother yelled from her bedroom in the back of the house.

What was going on?

Lulu shot toward the door. She stopped and took my face in her hands. They were hot and wet. I could smell her perfume under the damp weight of worry. She kissed me on the forehead and headed for her car without saying a word to me.

Mom emerged from the hallway, flustered and crying. She stopped and put a hand on the counter for balance, lifted a heel backwards and adjusted her shoe strap with the other hand. She slapped her shoe down on the linoleum, reached for her purse on the table and darted toward the same door bound for her sister's car.

She mimicked Lulu's behavior with me and said, "Something's wrong. We are going to Grandma's. You stay here."

She reached for the door.

"Can't I come?" I protested.

"No. Stay here. Stay in the house and listen for the phone."

She left and slammed the door behind her.

I wondered what could be happening. Was something wrong with Grandma? Or Grandpa? They weren't that old but I knew kids who had grandparents that got sick and died.

Was that it? Was Grandma sick and dying?

I could call Grandma's house.

208-42 ....

What was the phone number?

I remember Bridgette sitting at the kitchen table with me a few weeks ago, trying to help me memorize my grandparents' phone number. We saw them several times a week under normal circumstances. But if anything bad happened, we were to call Grandma or Grandpa first. Then Aunt Lulu and Uncle Ronaldo. Then Benny. Then Rick. Then Denny and Barbara from Utah. Then grandma Evelyn and her husband Dick. Then after that, Bridgette... If she wasn't already with us. That was the order of things. My mother created that order. Usually Dad knew exactly what to do. In this sort of instance my mother knew what to do.

Bridgette pulled Cheerios one at a time from the store box and shaped numbers on the table while I ate similar ones with sugar and milk. She formed numbers with the cereal. It was her way of helping me learn the best numbers to call where people would know what to do.

I was glad she was always there.

I never learned her number.

What if I remembered the rest of the numbers to call Grandma's house and I called and she were dying when the phone rang? I couldn't bare to talk with her if she were dying. Mom and Lulu hadn't had sufficient time to get there. So if Grandma were dying it would be up to her or Grandpa to get the phone. Grandpa never answered the phone. If I called would Grandpa answer and then I would know? I would know that Grandma was truly in a bad way.

But, if Grandma answered would that mean that she and Grandpa were just fine?

What if it was neither of them?
What if it was their only son? My uncle.

Wade.

What if it was Wade?

Three days later, on Friday, relatives I had only heard of but never met, began filling my grandparents' green and white trailer home. One of them was an "Uncle" Charlie from a famous country band. The cramped trailer became an obit truck stop that night.

My uncle had died.

Last summer I sat in the passenger seat of his silver 1970 Pontiac Trans Am. He washed it in the front yard of Grandma and Grandpa's rented red brick home.

The garden hose lay running in the grass. Wade pushed in an 8 track tape. The Rolling Stones blared into the street, filling the neighborhood with expectations. Mothers along the block could hear the sound of anger in the music that washed through their screen doors like rain.

I sat in the car with the doors open. Uncle Wade was hosing and wiping. Hosing and wiping.

He smoked his cigarette and smiled proudly at his clean car. Like all other summers, that one was endless.

Uncle Wade was returning home from boot camp.

It was late at night. He had stopped to help an older couple who had run out of gas. He drove them to the nearest gas station and returned them to their stranded car. The woman returned to her place in the passenger seat. Wade and her husband stood outside chatting while they poured fuel from a can into the gas tank.

According to police, a young man driving his car under the influence of "booze and dope" came up over the hill at about eighty miles an hour and clipped the two men.

Picked like April cherries.

In the months and years that followed the tragedy, after the shock and sorrow of my Uncle's death melted from icy memory, I often considered the awful scene that belonged to the old woman in the car. Left alone in the dark, the soft silence of death whirling around her in hopeless little gusts.

The driver door ripped from its hinges and and lost somewhere ahead on the asphalt.

My young Uncle and her old husband swept away like scraps.

Two men in disparate parts of a dirty path, landed hard on the same stretch of strange highway.

My Grandparents' trailer was small. I didn't imagine so many people could fit in it. My Grandmother was one of twenty-one children. Many of them were there that night.

Cigarette smoke hung over the small kitchen and living room like curtains, drifting and swaying over an open window. The uncle Charlie had a guitar under his arm. I had never seen so many open bottles of brown liquor. I recognized one of the bottles. Whiskey.

I sat on the sofa and watched the addled emotion slosh around the room like water in a kiddie pool. Charlie strummed his guitar and sang a few verses of a familiar song and then stopped. He held a half full bottle of whiskey high above his head, looked into the face of my Grandmother, and started to speak, but his words turned into sad laughter and he drank from the bottle.

Most everyone in the room followed suit.
My Grandfather sat at the far end of the kitchen table. He had a glass that was nearly empty. He was void of any expression. It was as if he had gone to wherever Wade was. His only boy was dead. Maybe Grandpa died for a time.

Grandma came to the sofa and sat down next to me. I didn't know what drunk felt like but I knew what it looked like. She slumped over and laid her head in my lap. This was opposite of normal. I recognized the weakness that was lying in someone's lap. She wasn't crying but she should have been. She was rambling about how I was part of her clan and how proud she was of me and that everything was going to be fine and that she was sure of it.

I looked up for help. Mom had gone home earlier with Aunt Lulu. My father was sitting next to Grandpa at the kitchen table. There were so many bodies moving around that I could only catch brief glimpses of him now and then.

I was on my own. This was the beginning.

It would always be on me to catch the heavy heads and wounded hearts.

Uncle Wade's funeral service was held at a nearby Mormon Church. Wade wasn't Mormon. Grandma and Grandpa weren't Mormon. There were only a couple of Mormons in the family. When it came to matters of a spiritual nature, they always needed things to be done by their rules.

Whoever planned my Uncle's funeral decided it would be a desirable emotional spectacle to have the youngest, most emotionally fragile members of the family sing a church song as an homage to our lost Uncle.

A couple of days before the service, a short round woman with large bosoms and horn-rimmed prescription glasses came to our home where she lead me, my sister Paris, and three of my female cousins through the rehearsal of a long and tortuous hymn entitled, "I Wonder When He Comes Again."

The day of the service, upon queue, the five of us made our way to the front of the chapel. We stood near the pulpit in our assigned order. The organ played and we sang the words we rehearsed. Soon we were all crying and struggling to finish the song. It was a satisfactory performance as the small congregation was entirely in tears. Except for the busty Mormon song leader. She was smiling with morbid joy. She almost seemed giddy with pride over our emotional performance.

If there is a god, he had other matters to attend to that day, because there was nothing warm or hopeful or redeeming about the moment we sent our beloved Uncle off into the perimeter.

My father had been coming home early from work a lot that summer.

We were due back at school in a few weeks.
His friends were around less and less.
The house was much less clean and orderly.
The lawn was shaggy.

Something was wrong.
Not wrong like when Mom had one of her episodes.
Something was really wrong.

Late one night my father woke in excruciating pain.
I could hear him groaning from where I lay in my concrete quarters in the basement. There was some shuffling and some quiet commotion and then shoes traversing the kitchen floor above me. The back door opened and then closed. The car started and I sat straight up in bed. The sound of the engine grew louder as the car passed my bedroom window framed near the rafters above my bed. The metal hasp rattled with the motor. The car quickly rolled down the drive.

I sat breathless for a moment. I was unsure what was happening and what I was supposed to do.

Then I heard another quiet commotion in another part of the house above me.

Footsteps were headed toward the kitchen and then down the stairs toward me. It was Paris. I knew the intonation of all of the feet in my family.

She came into my room and sat down next to me. "Don't be worried. Dad felt sick and Mom decided to take him to the doctor."

"Right now? In the middle of the night? Can't they wait till tomorrow?"

"No," she said. "He was really feeling sick and didn't want to wait till tomorrow."

A car with a loud engine sped down the road and past the house. We both looked up to the window as the headlights flickered through the glass.

"When will they be back?" I asked.

"They won't be very long. The doctor will probably just give him a little medicine and then they'll come home. Don't worry."
She rubbed my back in quick short strokes.

"Can I sleep with you?" I whined.

"Do your feet stink?" She asked.

The whining continued. "Noooooo. Paris, please let me sleep with you."

"Ok. Come on."

We ran up the stairs. She was faster than I was. I hated being last up the stairs. I always had that feeling that someone was coming up behind me. Chasing me. It gave me a thrilling and frightening tingling sensation in my toes. Just like when I stood on a high balcony and looked down. Just like when I watched parachuters on tv as they threw themselves from small planes.

Many years later, my father would marry a woman half his age. My step-mother leapt from a fifth story window. I wondered if she got that same feeling in her feet.

Paris' bed was bigger than mine. I asked if I could sleep against the wall. The evening was cool and the house was old and quiet. This particular July, the nights were a certain sort of chilly.

I never felt safer than when I was close to my sister.

Unlike my father, I understood her. Unlike my mother, I trusted her. Unlike anyone else, she loved me.

She loved me in the most visceral way. She cared that I slept and that I ate and that I was warm and that I wasn't frightened.

We covered up and tried to get settled in. We fell asleep with our backs together and our knees pulled close to our bellies.

The next morning everything was different. I didn't know it yet. I wouldn't know it for a few years. Our story. Our map. It was all being rewritten.

All of the summer vacations and Christmas parties and spring gardening and cupboards full of food. All of it would change. All of it would soon be remarkably absent.

The things I'd made into memories that shifted and mutated and malformed into an illusion of so many happy times... They somehow slipped out of my bedroom window that night and danced into the darkness with the flickering headlights.

I could smell coffee.

Dad was ok. He was ok. It was fine. Everything was fine. Things were ok. Normal. Dad was in the kitchen just like every morning. He was making coffee. Soon, I would hear the shower go on and after the water stopped running I would hear Dad humming some tune from the radio while he dressed. Then I would hear him in the kitchen cupboard looking for his coffee cup. He would turn the radio on and he would sit at the table, perusing the paper while sipping his coffee.

Then he would go to work and when he came home, Benny and Uncle Ronaldo and Bridgette would come by and they would pour drinks and light their cigarettes and put on a record and Mom would come out and dance with Bridgette and the front door would stay open late into the night and all of this would be proof that everything was going to be ok.

I sat up and looked around. Paris wasn't in the bed next to me. I threw the covers back and made for the bedroom door. When I got to the kitchen, Paris was pouring coffee into a cup. Dad's cup. Why was she using Dad's cup?

I surveyed the room. My father wasn't there. I couldn't smell his after shave or the soapy clean steam coming from the bathroom down the hall.

"Do you want some cereal?" Paris asked me while she stirred the cup of coffee with a spoon.

I issued an unenthusiastic, "Yea."

"I'll be right back."

She passed me holding the hot cup by the handle and went to Mom and Dad's bedroom door and knocked gingerly.

"Dad? Mom?"

She turned the knob and walked in. I could hear Dad take a deep breath. Like it was his first of the day.

"Dad, I brought you coffee."

"I just made it. It's hot."

My father's voice was quiet. Meek.

"Thank you, Paris. Where's your brother?"

"He's in the kitchen. I'm going to make him some cereal. Do you want some?"

"No. Thank you. I'm getting up now."

"Do you feel better from last night?"

"Yea. A bit."

I could hear him making grunting noises. Like he was working at something. I heard him opening a drawer.

Paris re-emerged from their room. She was happy. Perhaps just happy with herself for being a successful caretaker. Or maybe she was happy because things would be fine and she knew it.

"What kind of cereal do you want? We have Raisin Bran and Cheerios."

"I want Cheerios with lots of sugar."

I sat at the table. There were sticky drink rings on the table. Paris had her back to me. She was in cut-off shorts and a white cotton shirt with puffy short sleeves and colored embroidery on the front. I was still in pajamas. The Cheerios made tiny bell sounds as they hit the bottom of the bowl.

Dad suddenly appeared from the hall. He was in pressed jeans and a casual shirt. He walked with an uncomfortable gait. He was trying to hide a grimace on his face. I was staring intently at him. He knew it. I couldn't stop though. I wanted to. I didn't want to see him like this. It wasn't that he looked awful or disgusting. He just wasn't the man I was used to. His steps were lighter. His voice was softer. His eyes didn't look through my goddamned soul.

This was only temporary. He got some medicine at the hospital.

"Did they give you medicine at the hospital, Dad?"
I inquired.

"Yes, Son. They gave me medicine."

"Is it the flu?"

"Yes, its like the flu."

This was just for now. It wouldn't last long. My father feared nothing. He was stronger than anyone I knew. This soft man wincing in the kitchen without his boots on was not my father.
This was just a visitor.

A mosquito that had crept in through a torn screen.
An irritation.

My father would squash this. He would know exactly how to handle this.

He eased into a chair next to me at the kitchen table. Paris set the bowl of cereal in front of me. I began to feed.

I disliked Cheerios when they became soft.
The meter was running.

"Son, go get my boots for me."

I had just filled my mouth with crispy cereal. Time was so-goddamned-of-the-essence. These were thoughts only for thinking. Not for speaking. Even if my father were riddled with bullet holes, you wouldn't talk back to him. He'd still knock Monday through Friday out of you. He could be on his deathbed and he'd leave you barely a weekend.

I slipped down under the table and ran off to his bedroom for his boots.

"Don't disturb your mother!"

"I won't!"

When I got to the end of the hall, I slowed down and lit my feet a little more softly on the gold and brown shag carpeting.

I opened the bedroom door slowly. The moment I cracked the door I could smell my mother. Her morning smell was always slightly repulsive to me. A mix of bad breath and sour skin. A subtle staleness. I pushed my head into the breach and everything became warmer and damper and I wanted to hold my breath.

I'd only been inside a couple of times.
It wasn't that it was a holy place or that my parents were worried that we might break something valuable in my mother's musty little parcel of ruin.

It was that there was an intimacy to my mother's suffering.

That was where she cut herself open and let her devils spill out into the sheets and onto the floor. All of her naked wounds unseen and salted kept her carefully in her suburban tomb.

We were expected to show reverence.

I quietly made my way to the closet. Mom stirred.
I carefully reached into the open closet and picked up my father's boots. He had several pair. Some were for night time. I knew which ones he wore out in the day time. They were heavy and fashioned of black leather.

He kept a pair of thin black socks balled up in the left boot. Always.

I turned and headed toward the door. Mission nearly accomplished.

"Chuck? Come here sweetie."

My mother's tiny bell voice.
I turned to see her arm extended from under the covers, her fingers wiggling expectantly.

"Come heeeere."

Dad said not to bother her. I feared him more than I feared rejecting my mother.

"Sweetieeee."

I went to her side. She fumbled for my hand. The rest of her body was still. Her head deeply set on its side in the pillow. She stared at my eyes.

She spoke sadly. "How are you?"

"I'm fine." I responded.

I tried to pull my hand away. Dad would be expecting his boots. She gripped my hand more tightly.

"Why are you leaving?" She whined.

"I have to take Dad his boots."
"Why does he need his boots? Where is he going?"

"To work, Mommm."

"He can't work. He's sick."
"He got medicine from the doctor. He's better. I have to go. He needs his boots, Mom."

"Come and give me a kiss first, Chuck."

She pulled me toward her. I bent down to kiss her cheek. Her breath was sour. She lifted her head just enough to show effort.

I pecked her cheek and made a smacking sound.

I got to the kitchen where Dad and Paris were talking about school. I disliked that subject.

I hastily delivered my Father's boots at his feet. In no time he was out the door.

You see? Nothing could stop my father.

I finished my cereal. Paris played in her room and the house was still. I could hear none of the neighbor boys in the street. I cleaned my spoon in one slick motion with tight lips and set it on the table. I lifted the cereal bowl to my mouth with both hands and began drinking the sugary milk. This was my favorite part of breakfast.

I poured too fast and spilled some down one side of my face. I set the bowl down and wiped my mouth on my shoulder.

There was a tiny drop of milk forming on the bowl's edge where my mouth was. It was terribly small and I fixed on it. The tiny white orb was forming with a delicate tremble to it. As if it were a new little planet being launched into an unwanted trajectory.

The brown wooden table beneath it lay cold and dark like an old galaxy pulling the droplet downward. It shuttered and shimmered in the morning light. Then, a thin thread formed between the droplet and the bowl and finally snapped. The orb was cut loose and fell to the table.

I smeared at it with my forefinger and carried my bowl and spoon to the sink. I didn't wash them. Paris would likely do it today.

I drifted through the day without purpose or desire. Wandering the yard. Staring across the road to the ballpark and the public pool where some of the taller kids were climbing the ladder to the high dive. We had lived in the house for just over a year and I had never been to the public pool. I stood in the back yard leaning, belly first, into the chain-link fence and gazed across the road at the splashing and squawking. Like goslings in a pond.

I climbed the tree and sat on a slat of wood nailed into an upper branch--a failed attempt at a treehouse from beginning of the summer.

One of the nails had fallen out so that the slat spun like a propeller unless you placed yourself directly over the nail and sat cautiously. I wanted to build a spacious and clever tree house like I had seen in a Boys-Life magazine or on the TV or something. But I quickly realized that I lacked most of the necessary tools and hardware and that the tree would require pruning beyond my skill level.

I didn't know how to build things.

Even in the moment that I was building things as small boys do with their limited understanding and a load of ambition, I still realized I was a fool. In that exact moment, I would tell myself, "You don't know what exactly to do here. You are a fool."

I looked straight up through the branches and leaves into the warm afternoon sky.

The top of the old chestnut wore a summer shawl of broad green leaves that seemed like craft room cut-outs against the bright indigo sky. There were soft gusts of wind chasing through the leaves so that their shadows danced across my face. I closed my eyes and waited for the occasional beam of sunlight to land on my skin. I could feel the sturdy branch beneath me sway.

It reminded me of last summer when I rode an elephant at the Salt Lake City Zoo. My parents paid for the tickets and lead me with my sister to a small wooden staircase. There was a thin black man with a denim shirt and a red bandana tied in a knot around his bare neck standing at the top. He had beads of sweat all over his happy face.

He signaled us enthusiastically to climb the stairs. He was steadying an elephant and encouraging us to get up in the colorfully woven saddle with what looked like a metal frame around it.

I looked back at both of my parents faces. They seemed to feel it was a good idea. I stopped on the first of three or four steps and waited while the man helped my sister up on the mammoth creature. He happily ordered her to hold on to the metal bars that framed the saddle. Then he turned to me.

"Come on, boy!"
He waved me up. I obeyed and he put his hands under my arms and lifted me up and set me behind my sister.

I immediately wrapped my arms around her waist and joined my hands together as tightly as I could. I delved into my emotions hoping to discover excitement but I could only manage to find fear. A grungy, young man lead the elephant with a thick rope.

His huge legs began a slow and lumbering march. I lay the side of my face on my sister's back and held her more tightly. The smell of the animal reminded me of rotting wood or wet lawn trimmings.

I sat silent on the branch while it lumbered in the breeze. I knew I was safe. The old tree was sure footed.

I opened my eyes and glanced at the ground beneath me. I was too close to the ground. I looked back up through the waving canopy of leaves.

I wanted to be up there. Closer to the unknown.
I wanted to feel safe further from the earth.

I adjusted my footing and shimmied further up the large branch. Climbing a tree was something I knew how to do. I did it better than any of the boys in the neighborhood.

With little effort, I made it to a clearing. Nothing but sunshine. The branch rocked much more up here.

I looked down.
I was perhaps ten feet higher than a moment ago. My warm skin raised between the fear that had crawled up underneath it and the cool wind that exhaled across it.

I found a perfect seat high up on the branch where I could see everything.

I could see the neighbor boy, Gary, playing in his back yard. He had no idea I was here.
I was invisible to the world.

Mrs. Kirby was hanging laundry in her back yard.
She was pretty and always seemed happy. If she ever looked me in the face, I felt my face get hot and red.

I had a perfect view of the public pool across the street. I got lost for a long time in my private world in the tree. Then I saw an old man slowly making his way up the sidewalk adjacent to the park. He was dressed like old men dress. He wore a Trilby hat, creased slacks, and a short-sleeved dress shirt. His gait was slow and steady. His hands in his pockets. He mostly looked down at the ground as he walked.
I thought of the elephant again.

Three crows lit on a line at the edge of our yard. They watched the old man and chattered with one another. One took off and flew low over the old man and cried. He circled and returned to his friends on the power line. What business did they have with the old man?

Everything was moving more slowly now. I had been staring at the crows for so long that they were becoming black paper cut outs. The old man disappeared.
He hadn't noticed me on my perch.

But I saw him. I saw his gray sideburns peeking out from under the rim of his hat. I saw the wrinkled skin on his arms. It hung from his wooden bones like old wallpaper. I watched the crows nag at him until he was gone. Like an old satellite falling out of orbit. Like an elephant at the end of a thick rope.

I would never feel safe in this heavy sway with lonely old men and cut-out crows. I wanted to forget that I saw him. I wanted to move the memory away or hide it. Like covering a dead bird so you don't have to see it.

You move more slowly in warm water.

It feels better around your skin than cold water does. But it's a delicate mind-fuck. Swimming in warm water you become fooled into believing you belong there. You pretend to be elegant and graceful with your skin and bones thrashing underwater. You imagine you're part of a magical journey. You've connected with something foreign to you.

Water.

But you will drown.

Soon, you'll soften your strokes and just like your first kiss, you'll close your eyes and take a deep breath. You'll fill your fragile lungs with a polar, inorganic compound. Before you can choke, you'll have smothered yourself in foolishness and salt water.

My father seemed to be improving. I don't know if he was simply getting used to his pain or if he was actually getting better.

I think he was just starting to swim in warm water.

Summer was over. The days were still warm but the nights were cooler and we didn't trounce in the streets in our bare feet any longer. We didn't get sweaty heads or grass stains as much. My sister and I were back in school and the neighbor kids mostly disbanded.

Paris and I didn't get back-to-school clothing that year. Mom said we'd get some school clothes in a few weeks when Dad got paid.

"What the hell is wrong with you? I'm sorry you don't feel well. None of us feel well! Stop being so selfish! Your kids are depending on you! They need clothes and school supplies!"

That was the year my father bought me a plastic supplies box at the Sears on Overland Avenue. It was a lightweight, blue case with an opaque lid. It was like grandpa's tackle box but easier to carry. Dad bought me a handful of pencils and a pink, square eraser to go inside. At school, I kept it inside my desk with the heavy wooden lift top. During class, I would frequently lift the desktop to look at my supplies box. It smelled like rubber and lead and made me feel able.

Mrs. Taylor was my teacher. She was tall and slender and had dark hair stacked on her head. She wore matching wool skirts and jackets. She had a skirt suit for everyday of the week. She had freckles and kind, hazel eyes.

She liked me. She was always complimentary of my work. I wished I could stay in her classroom all day and evening.

I even imagined her as my mother.
She was smart and vibrant. Not pathetic and small.

That time of year was filled with angst and promise. It was getting colder but we had sweaters and the school had an old furnace that smelled like old books and hot metal. Mrs. Taylor made us feel comfortable and warm.

Every afternoon Paris and I would walk the few blocks home with friends and talk about the homework we'd been assigned and the strange janitor who smelled like cat piss and cigarettes.

I assume every child that becomes a kid is self-aware. I was a boy and, therefore, was only able to think like a boy. While I didn't think it at the time, there must have been a difference between the way boys and girls thought about themselves and their place in the big and colorful and confusing American world in the seventies. Every twenty or thirty years a generation becomes iconic. Not because of people or politics or art and music, but because ALL of those things are like gasoline on our hearts and then every twenty or thirty years someone lights a goddamned match.

And boom.

Boys wrestle with their masculinity and their worth and their place in the world. Girls claw at the putrid advances of the boys and all of this starts on sidewalks when we're all just becoming kids and laughing at each other and agreeing that the new librarian is fat. All the brown grass that helps make up an Autumn plaid with the concrete walks under the rotting apple trees is a quiet pattern that stays behind when winter comes.

We arrive home to the smell of roasts and cigarette smoke and warmth and stereos filling the air with words and sounds that would define our seventies sadness.

In the Fall of 1973 my father bought a Ford Galaxy for less than $4000. He stopped at the market and paid twenty-five cents for a dozen eggs and some bacon on the cheap. Nick, at the local gas station filled my father's tank for less than $9.

Dad came home and made me and my sisters breakfast for dinner.

Not a day has passed that I haven't thanked a god I've never believed in for my father. He held our messy little family together with pancakes and Linda Rondstadt and a little whiskey for himself.

He and Paris would clean the dishes and we'd settle in the living room with the TV and he'd watch the news and I could see his face pulling tightly around his eyes and lips. I didn't know who Jane Roe was. But he seemed pleased that Henry Wade lost. Dad had nothing good to say about Texas.

I was a boy then. I didn't really know much else.
I knew only that I was a floundering boy. I studied my father's face for clues. Because I knew I was drowning.
I watched his eyes like they were nautical charts.
I watched his lips around his cigarette and his throat that strained when he was angry with me and I began learning to manipulate and manage people because I studied my father so closely and I saw how the delicate nuances of his face instructed me to intimidate people and taught me to hide most everything I felt.

My father found his way back to cold water. That time period wasn't written by me or measured by the chapters herein. That period was already written by Nixon and Chrysler and Marvin Gaye and Jim Croce and Vietnam and Agnew and Billie Jean King.

I was the perfectly conditioned and lost, self-aware and most analytically inept non-coastal boy of the seventies. My parents weren't directors or authors or celebrities and there would be no legacy or inheritance for me.

I was it. When I finally figured that out, I was filled with panic. That's when the water dreams got worse. That's when I began cursing.

My Father and Uncle Ronaldo pronounced it "Son ova bitch." My Grandfather pronounced it "Son uffa bitch."

I was unsure which was most correct. Regardless, I chose that as my first foray into swearing. I used my Grandfather's redaction. At first I used it quietly, by myself. As if I were practicing. I listened to how it sounded and how it felt coming from my mouth. I would discover later that it tasted better on angry lips. I began using it in front of friends.

"Glenn Burton is a son uffa bitch," I would say to our mutual friend, Robbie Bowers. Robbie would laugh heartily at my language. Soon it became comfortable for both of us to curse between us. He seemed to like the word 'shit.' 'Son uffa bitch' seemed more manly and like a greater commitment to me. It left a more permanent echo in my ears. It placed me on a faster track to manhood.

My mother encouraged me to play with the Mormon boys from school. Robbie and Glenn were Mormon. We started walking to and from school together. We would rendezvous two blocks from my house on the corner in front of Robbie's house. We never walked straight to school. We most frequently found a little trouble to tie us up first. Glenn had a bevy of useful curse words and he was fluent in his use of them.

One morning, late in the fall, when it was cold enough for snow and there were still a few persistent leaves holding hard to their branches, we turned left on the old school road instead of right and headed toward the canal. There was an big tree that hung over the deep water where we climbed and yelled and cursed while the dark cold water rolled smooth, like glass under us.

Someone had left a pornographic magazine near the base of the tree. I jumped from a low-lying branch and landed in a layer of leaves near the magazine. I bent down and stared at it for a moment. I looked around. Robbie and Glenn were on a large branch out over the canal.

I brushed some dirt and leaves off the wrinkled pages. I carefully pinched the corner of a page with my forefinger and thumb and turned it uncomfortably.

On the following page was a series of photos of a beautiful blonde woman with unnaturally large, round, naked breasts sitting with her legs wide open in the back seat of a nice convertible sports car. Her lower body was also bare. She had a dark pubic scrub between her legs and a man with long sideburns and and a nice suit on was kissing her in the thicket between her thighs.

Each of the photos was a slightly different scene. They changed positions for the photographer several times to show mostly different angles of the woman's body.

The photos made me feel things I couldn't explain. Things in my head and in my chest and in other places I was certain I wasn't supposed to be feeling things. I stood up and turned away from the images.

I adjusted my underwear under my cords and yelled at Robbie and Glenn.

"Hey, you guys! Let's get out of here! We're going to be late for school! Hurry!"

Glenn always had a smart response to everything.

"Who cares! Don't be a pussy! It doesn't matter! My mom doesn't care if I'm late!"

My father WOULD care. Paris would care.

"C'mon! We'll come back after school!"

Robbie scrambled down the big branch toward the trunk and made his way down. He was anxious to leave too.

"Hey, Glenn. Me and Charles are leaving! You commin with us?"

Glenn was annoyed but he leapt from the big branch and landed on the bank just a couple of feet from the water and scurried up the bank and ran past us. He taunted us, yelling over his shoulder.

"C'mon you fairies! I'll beat you there!"

Robbie and I chased after.

These were our mornings.
They were moments of freedom that we stole from our parents and teachers. Those in betweens where we were expected, but not yet.

Those were the moments where, from the pre-pubescent mouths of Mormon boys, I learned about sex and girls and hunting with wrist rockets and how to burp louder and longer and how to steal eggs from the market to throw at cars later.

They were the first boys I smoked cigarettes with.
That same day, we were exploring an abandoned house. I had matches I had taken off the kitchen table that morning. We found some newspaper and rolled the pages up in our hands like snowballs and lit them on fire to throw into the basement windows. Glenn said there were Bawl Cats down there. We were only trying to light up the dark basement so we could see them.

So later the fire department came and so did my Father and Glenn's mother. We confessed that we had been smoking and then got the idea to throw fireballs into the house.

My father had a firm grip on my collar. Much like how a lion grabs a cub at the top of his neck with his teeth. Firm enough to hold, but not so hard as to kill.

He held me firmly in his jaws all the way home. He led me to my room where he set me on the edge of my bed.

"Don't move."

He left the room. He was unusually calm. I was confused. He wasn't yelling. He hadn't hit me yet.

He returned to my room and sat down next to me on the edge of my bed. He had an opened pack of cigarettes and a book of matches. He put a cigarette in his mouth and lit it. He was fluid in his motions. He didn't struggle at all trying to light the cigarette. It was second nature to him.

He took a deep drag and exhaled with his closed eyes pointed toward the ceiling. Then he removed the cigarette from his mouth, pinched theatrically between his forefinger and thumb like he was making the 'okay' sign with his hand, and told me to have a drag.

I didn't understand. I stared at the cigarette. Was this a trick? Was it a test? If I said no, would he punish me? If I took a drag, would he get angry? He would likely beat me no matter what I did.

I looked up at his face. He knew I was looking for clues.

"In fact, you take this one. I'll have my own."

He pushed it toward my face. I took the cigarette. I held it with my eyes fixed on it while my Father put a cigarette in his mouth and lit it. He inhaled and exhaled the same way as before.

My grip on the cigarette was far less graceful than his. I held is as if it were a dart I was about to throw. He could smoke alone. He was confident and strong and didn't need anyone to smoke with him. But if my father told you to do something, you damned well did it.

So I put the cigarette to my lips and pulled on it just a little. I had little experience with smoking. But I knew that beyond the social superiority that accompanied it, it was mostly unpleasant. I pulled a bit through the filter and coughed.

I held the cigarette away from my face while I cleared my lungs and burning eyes.

My father laughed and I wiped burning salt water from my eyes and grappled for better oxygen and my youthful pride. I didn't want my father to see me as weak.

He was good at this.

I was still learning how to hold my hands and how to cross my legs and how to smile with a careless set of cheekbones and arrogant teeth and how to fill my lungs with the right amount of smoke and how to billow like a perfectly plumb chimney and how to fill the evening air with confidence and father and son expressions that might make us equals for just a moment.

I felt dizzy. My father went on about the first time he smoked. He elbowed me and shouldered me and nudged me while he laughed and rambled and smoked and I stumbled into an awful and dizzy place. My mouth watered and tasted like tobacco and I knew I would soon disappoint my father again.

I felt his heavy hand on my shoulder. My head spun and I slipped off the edge of my mattress.
I had to get to the toilet.

I stumbled across the gold sculptured shag carpeting and fell to my hands. My neck cocked and my chin pointed toward the carpet and I saw the lunch lady through all of my guttural clumsiness. Then I was swirling stomach bile with my clumsy fingers while my tears mixed with all of the disgust that coated the carpeting.

My parents had always helped me when I was sick.
But this was a new world now.

I had never been drunk. But I felt drunk. My head spun while it hung low like and old, tired cow. My father's heavy feet walked across my bile and I knew I had become a man. I knew he wouldn't return with a warm, soapy cloth. I knew it was I that would have to clean up my clumsiness.

So I did.

I went to the kitchen and opened the cupboard door under the sink. I found a rag and some blue spray and returned to my smoke-filled room where I got on my knees and rubbed my vomit with ammonia cleaner and a piece of frayed bath towel.

*That winter played the same cold chords and it's
strange that we so easily remember the dance.*

We remember the order of decay like a song. We talk
about the color of the trees and the coolness of the air
and predict what winter will bring. We pull out the
boxes of scarves and hats and dig in lower drawers for
sweaters and we pine over soups and meat and our
autumn bones ache for new affection and we wrap our
clumsy arms around those we think will love us.

When we wake up in the Spring, we find our dreams
melting into sensational rivets. They carve sparkling
paths through a new season and into hopeful valleys
where we drown every goddamned year. We forget
how to swim. We forget that we can't breathe under
water and we become lost in the cool thaw.

That spring, my Father worked less and less. Our lives
were slowly becoming more fragile and shell-like.

My mother was sleeping more. We didn't have friends
over anymore.

We ate less from the stove and more from the cupboard. The yard let go. The neighbors peeked through the windows. The post piled up.

My sister, Paris worked to keep up on the general cleanliness and order of the house. I did little but wander in the narrows that filled all this new nothingness.

That was my purpose: to stumble into my accidental future. To fall dizzy to my knees into my own vomit and trace my fingers in the bile and the shag until I had mapped something I understood. Summer came and it meant nothing. My sister held our family together while I looked for the right route.
I never really understood how things worked.

My father had always...
Well...
That didn't matter anymore.

In 1982 I finished my junior year at Madison High in Rexburg, Idaho.

My sister had gone off to marry Prince Charming and I was left to map out my new manhood.

My father had been in and out of the hospital for the past several years. He had been diagnosed with Crohn's disease. In the early eighties the medical geniuses of the West were still trying to figure out how treat the disease. A few years earlier, they removed some of his small intestine and performed a partial bowel resection.

He had become angrier and more bitter than ever.
He disliked appearing weak or incapable. He wanted to work and provide for his family. So he'd work hard for a few weeks and then he'd have a bad bout and lay up for a week or so. His quality of life had diminished to something one could barely call a life.

He was on one of his upswings in the sickness cycle. He had decided we should go somewhere new. Apparently, Salt Lake City seemed a good choice.

It was the closest big city to Rexburg. There was plenty of work to be had. And my Uncle and Aunt lived there with their four daughters. We could land with them until we got a living arrangement sorted out. My mother and two younger sisters would remain home while my father and I went ahead to work, save money, and find a place to live.

Dad enrolled me at Bountiful High School.
These weren't my people. They all came from affluent families. Blonde boys with their Izod collars up and pleated khaki pants. Girls with fluffy eighties hair and shirts identical to the boys.

The school was larger than any school I'd seen. One could get lost in it. And I did. I struggled to acclimate. My cousins were all pretty girls who fit in very well. They introduced me to a few people. I made one or two good friends with whom I'd finish out my school days.

I was in school four weeks when my father said we were going home for the weekend. We did. While we were there my father told my mother to start packing and that he and I would return in two weeks to move our family to Salt Lake. This was great news. It wasn't that I missed my mother and younger sisters. It was that I missed our normal. Everything was on the up and up. Things were going to be just fine.

On Sunday afternoon we said our goodbyes and Dad and I jumped in his work van and headed out of town. We stopped for gas outside of Rexburg and Dad said he was tired and asked if I would drive.

"Of course!" I said.

He told me what signs to watch for in case he dozed off and he reclined his seat and fell asleep.

I had the radio volume on low. Hall & Oates played and the windows were down. It was September in the high desert. It was warm, and the whole world was framed by a dirty windshield while it glowed gold and green. I could smell fuel and sage and dirt and my chest filled with so much hope and desire for this to be our new normal.

I was driving.
And my father was napping in the passenger seat. He trusted me. He finally knew I could handle things. I'm sure I was smiling while I rested my wrist on the wheel at 12 o'clock. I bobbed my head and mouthed the words to the song on the radio.

"Don't you KNOWWWW? Don't YOU knowww?"

An hour or so later, my father began making noises in his sleep. At first I thought he was dreaming. After several minutes, I realized he was in pain and his noises coincided with flinching while his hand grabbed at his gut.

I was watching him while trying to watch the road.
I wasn't sure what to do.

"Dad. Are you ok?"

He didn't respond. Was he dreaming? I didn't understand. I wasn't sure what to do.

He began thrashing about. He moaned in pain.
He called my name.

"Charlie!"

"Yea, Dad. Are you ok? What should I do?"

"Find a hospital!" He yelled through gritted teeth.

No. No. No. I didn't know how to handle this. We were in the middle of nowhere. I told my father to hold on. I throttled it. I was doing almost 90 across the desert. I could see a sign ahead.

Shit. SHIT SHIT SHIT! Pocatello was the next major city and it was fifty miles out.

My Father writhed and cried next to me. I held his hand and he squeezed it so hard I thought he'd break it. He was always the strongest man I knew. He had such strong hands. Those hands at the end of sinuous arms had hurt me and protected me on many occasions.

I tried to console him. I told him we were almost there. We weren't. But I told him we were.

We came upon Pocatello and I saw a sign for a hospital. I took the exit and followed the signs. I raced into the lot of the clinic. I parked in a loop and told my father I'd be right back. I ran inside for help.

"Help me! Please help me! Help my Father! Please!"

A large woman in a floral smock came out from behind a counter.

"Where's your Father?"

"Out here. In the van."

I was crying now.
She followed me outside. I opened the passenger door and Dad nearly fell out.

He looked like a blind man who had lost his mind.

His arms were flailing around and we was grimacing and groaning.

I had never seen my father cry. He wasn't crying with tears. It was worse. He was only crying with his voice. I couldn't bear to hear it. I couldn't stand to see my Father like this.

"But. This. Is. Where. I. Am." I thought.
"You have to do this. This is on you."

I helped the woman in the smock shoulder my Father. We got him inside, through a set of double doors and into an emergency area with multiple beds. We got him to a bed and a man in green scrubs came to join the struggle. The man asked me question after question.

"What happened?"
"I don't know." I replied.

"Has he taken any drugs?"

"No! I mean... what kinds of drugs? He takes medicine."

"For what?" The man asked.

"For Crohn's disease."

"How long has he been in pain?"

"I don't know." I said. "Maybe an hour."

I was holding Dad's hand. The man told me to go out in the waiting area and that they would take care of my Father. I stood there and held his flinching hand.

"Don't worry," the man said. "We'll take care of your Dad."

I let go.

I found my way out to the waiting room.
I didn't know what to do. Would they give him some medicine and he'd be fine? Would he have to stay for a while? What would I tell my mother?

She wouldn't know what to do. She'd just wait until my Father told her what she should do. But what if he couldn't tell her?

I could occasionally hear my Father's groans through the double doors. I wanted to be away from the sounds and the sadness that I was hearing.

After a while, the large woman came through the double doors. She smiled kindly and said, "Your Dad is in a little pain but he's feeling better. We have him something for the pain. We're going to keep him overnight. Do you have someone you can call or somewhere you can stay?"

I looked at her confused. My eyes filled with tears. My face felt hot. I came apart. I cried and hid my face.

"Noooo. I don't know anyone here. My mom..."

I felt the big woman's arms around me. She smelled like roses but she wasn't familiar and I was embarrassed.

"Where's your mom, Honey?"

"In Rexburg." I said.

"Ohhhh. Oh my. Well. Why don't we give her a call."

"No. She won't do anything. She won't know what to do."

I tried to pull myself together. I wiped my messy face and dried my hands on my pants.
"Can I see my Dad?"

"Sure you can, Honey. Come with me."

She led the way back to the bed where my father was. She pulled the curtain back and my dad was lying there with a couple of wires attached to his finger and chest. He had some tape covering a cotton ball on his arm.

He looked and me and held out his hand. I broke down again and took his hand. He told me how sorry he was and that it must've been the tomato juice he had at the gas station or something. The big woman left and Dad and I talked for a few minutes about nonsense.
Then he said, "Let's get out of here."

"What? No, Dad. They want to keep you overnight."

"That's not happening, Son."

He struggled and sat up on the edge of the bed.
He pulled the monitors off his finger and chest.
He got to his feet and rested a hand on my shoulder.
We walked through the double doors and the woman and the man who had helped us were talking at the main desk.

"Hey!" Said the man. "Where you going?"

"I'm better," said my Dad. "We're going to go ahead and get back home now."

"Noooo. That's not a good idea." She responded.
"You need to be monitored overnight."

My Father replied, "I'm leaving. You can't stop me."

We made a hasty exit and got back in the van.
I turned it over.
"Dad, what should I do?"

"Let's go back home, Son. We'll sort it out from there."

I was due back at my new school in the morning.
How would we sort this out? I found my way back to
the highway and headed north.

Dad fell asleep. He wasn't in pain anymore. I was glad.
The golden green was becoming dark and cold now.

I cried most of the way back home. But I was thankful
my Father wasn't crying.

When we got back to Rexburg, Mom got dad settled into their bedroom so he could rest.

The two of them spoke quietly about all of it. They spoke with the door ajar and I could not hear what they whispered and cried about.

We were going to stay the course. Mom had contacted an agent who would be visiting the next day. The house would be listed by Wednesday and would sell for twelve thousand less than what my parents were asking. Within a couple of weeks a moving truck would back into the drive and our whole lives would become cargo with numbered stickers. Every memory listed on an inventory sheet with carbon copies to insure those memories arrived in a new and empty place.

A smiling Samoan Mormon with sinuous arms and a happy disposition delegated work to two other movers.

One was a tall, lean ginger, not much older than I. The other was a portly older man. Short with black, slicked-back hair.

The Samoan was confident and playful and had arms like Popeye. He moved our 1938 piano into the truck almost entirely alone.

Mom called out for pizza and cola for the movers and soon we were in Utah with our carbon copies and scuffed piano.

The church arranged for a rental for us in Centerville-- a northern suburb of Salt Lake. The place was odd.

It had an unkempt pool, which made it more damp and desperate going into a Salt Lake winter.

I can't really talk about this winter.

Not now, at least. If I've come undone, it might have been this winter that loosened the laces. The dirty pool stayed dirty. The cold nights stayed cold. And the Mormon neighbors stayed away.

I fell asleep that winter and woke in the spring like my mother had taught me. She was too busy hiding to teach me much. But she damn well taught me how to sleep through the hard seasons.

We were strange people living in a strange house.
I had driven my father across the high desert and watched him in his ache while he fumbled with small towns and their small ideas and kind nurses.

I had seen the whole of humanity in a half sort of way and now I was unplugging my hope and settling into settling. I was swallowing my medicine. Finally.

I was doing what my mother taught me to do.
And hiding from my Father.

He was suffering and angry and I couldn't bear to see him or to be seen by him. I forgave him and feared him. I plotted against him while I prayed for him. I wanted him to love me and I wanted him dead.

I was seventeen.
All of this made my bones soft and tired.

So I slept.
Just for that winter.
That's what I did.
I fell asleep that winter.
And I waited for spring.

When I woke up it was raining.

At first I thought it was a dream. The soft smell of sumac and mildew verve made me long for something I could hold on to. Something easier to write about later. Like hot concrete and petrichor.

Or dashing through the canyons in Saabs and Pugeots and old Audis with the windows gaping.

It rained most of that spring. What a goddamned racket the weather business was that year. It ruled all of the matters of my heart and mind. It wouldn't allow me to govern my emotions even if I knew how.

It seemed to manage me completely. It forced me to feel all the distant thunder in my chest and waited for me to weep with every storm that rolled across the mountains and into our sleep.

Dad found good work. He bought a new Toyota pick-up. He kept it unrealistically clean. He smoked in the cab but never used the ash tray.

It wouldn't stop raining.

The city was uneasy and seemed to be groaning under the weight of the weather.

One afternoon I was sitting on the front porch looking into the drenched streets and the green hills above our neighborhood. A small pickup rounded the corner at the bottom of the block. I heard the transmission shift into third gear. It was my father. He pulled into the drive. He jumped quickly out of the cab of his Toyota and told me to grab a jacket and rain boots. I obeyed.

He followed me into the house. I went downstairs to my damp room in our unfinished basement. I heard Dad's heavy footsteps above me.

He opened the door to his bedroom and I could hear his muted voice. He was talking to Mom. I heard one or two words from her tired mouth. I grabbed my stinky pipe-moving boots from the back of the closet.

I went back upstairs and into the kitchen. I opened a cupboard and grabbed a handful of soda crackers.
Dad appeared in the doorway of the kitchen.

"Let's go, Son."

We climbed in the truck and Dad put the stick in reverse and pulled into the deluge. A few minutes later we arrived at a house in a flatter part of town.

There was water nearly up to the door of the truck. Dad told me the house belonged to an old woman and we had to sandbag it for her. There were only a handful of sandbags.

"Bob Jensen is bringing more sandbags. He'll be here soon."

We rearranged some of the bags that were already there. I had no idea it was this bad. The water was moving rapidly, just below my knees. A few minutes passed and a large flatbed pulled up. Mr. Jensen and another man climbed down from the flatbed and shook my father's hand. My father called me over.

"C'mon, Son. Let's get these bags off the truck."

The four of us worked together and began placing sandbags around the old woman's house. I was physically strong and in good shape. Soon my hands began hurting and I was soaked from boot to bone.

The light in the sky was quickly being smothered by the night and the rain clouds. Suddenly, we heard sirens. Not police or fire engines. It was a siren I'd never heard. Loud and long and chilling. My father and the two men stood straight up and listened quietly.

"We've gotta get to higher ground now, boys."

Bob Jensen had some worry in his voice. He and the other man headed for the flatbed. We had unloaded all the sandbags but hadn't placed them all yet.

Bob climbed behind the wheel. The door was still open and he yelled at my father.

"Clyde! You and your boy get outta here!"

My father waved him away.

"We're fine. We'll finish up and head home."

Bob stared at my father like he was crazy. The large truck fired up and the diesel engine roared in the darkness. The power had been knocked out.

Dad turned on his headlights and pointed the truck toward the house. He didn't say a word to me.
He didn't have to.

At first I was scared. But then I got over it.

We worked quietly together. Only the sound of grunts and sloshing.

The sirens continued for several minutes and then fell silent. It was eerie. If my father wasn't worried then I wasn't worried. We built up a solid barrier around the old woman's front and back doors.

"Let's go, Son!"

He didn't have to say another word. I beat him to the pickup. He climbed in, shoved the truck into gear and we were off. The traffic lights were out most everywhere. We sped east toward the mountains hitting some deep water now and then on our way out of the valley.

We got home and pulled off our soggy jackets and boots. Dad flipped on the television. He wanted to check in with the news.

I went to the kitchen to round up some food. I was standing with the refrigerator door open and staring into the void like teenage boys do.

"Son! Come here!"

The news people were reporting that a levee had broken in the hills and that a lot of water was headed into the valley. Apparently, we got out of there just in time. He looked at me with a twinkle in his eye. It was as if he had cheated and not gotten caught. I felt a rush of excitement and pride.

We found out the next day that the old woman's house withstood the flood from the levee. Most of the houses near her were terribly damaged.

That was on them.
They were owned by men who could take care of themselves and their families.

The old woman fled the rising water and had gone to stay with her daughter further up the mountain. What kind of men would we be if she came home and found her long-time home demolished? What kind of men would we be if we didn't risk a little for someone who had so little.

Maybe my my father wasn't getting used to the warm water. Maybe he was swimming. Maybe he was teaching me to swim. Maybe he knew a thing or two about rising water that other men didn't know. Anyway, I was beginning to think I could learn something valuable from my father.

That was the spring I woke up.

The weather cleared and it was a brilliant summer in the high desert of Utah.

Dillon Madison and I became friends at the end of the school year. He was popular. A jock. But he had a dynamic personality and he was kind. I had grown tall and sinuous and my voice changed to the one I have now. Most of the boys were intimidated by me.

Some of the girls started paying attention to me.

School was out. I was glad. I enjoyed racing around town with Dillon in his father's sports car with U2 and Night Ranger and Def Leppard blaring through our open windows. We sang to David Bowie. We danced to Thriller. We wore mullets on our sunburnt heads. We sported sleeveless t-shirts with our favorite bands printed across our broad, young chests.

I was happy. It was my first realization that I was happy. At least... happy enough to define it and utter it in my head. Sometimes I even mouthed it.

That was usually when Dillon was racing north on 500 West Street, breaking the speed limit and I'd close my eyes while the sun and wind swept my heart up and whispered youthful summer secrets in my ears.

I'm happy.

That's what my mouth said without asking my voice for help.

Dillon introduced me to a beautiful girl. Mia Gray was a cheerleader. She was dark haired with dark, deeply set eyes that made her look Russian. She was curvy and smelled good. All of her friends were pretty. She acted like she liked me. I knew that wasn't real.
But I went along with it.

For a few days, she hung out with both me and Dillon. One evening, I was in my room listening to Detroit Rock City by Kiss on my record player. I heard my father yelling for me from the top of the stairs.
I poked my head out the door.

"Yea????"

"There's someone here for you!"

What? The only person who would be coming to see me would be Dillon. If it was Dillon, why didn't dad just say it was Dillon? Or why didn't he just send him down like always?

I climbed the stairs to the front door. Standing inside my house politely and quietly waiting for me was Mia Gray.

When she saw me she smiled. Goddammit, my heart was racing. What was she doing here? Was Dillon waiting out in the car? I was confused.

"Hey." Her voice was sweet and she looked like an angel standing in front of the screen door with the evening sun behind her.

I struggled to be cool. "Hey. What are your doing?"

She came toward me and hugged me and said, "I just walked down to see if you wanted to hang with me at my house."

Are you KIDDING ME? Of COURSE I wanted to, "Hang out? And do what?"

She laughed. "I've got a lot of records. I thought we could listen to music and talk."

My father was sitting at the dining room looking over bills. He looked up and I saw a little smile on his face.

"Dad, is it ok if I go to Mia's house for a bit?"
He was as soft as I'd seen him. "Yes. Home by ten."

With that, we were out the door. We walked the several blocks to Mia's house. We talked about our day and she laughed at me and acted like she liked me.
I went along with it.

When we arrived at her house her parents weren't there. We went to the living room.

She had a nice stereo. She asked what I liked to listen to. I told her to choose. I wanted to see what she liked.

She pulled Fleetwood Mac from the rack and queued it up. We sat for hours and talked about music and school and friends and family. We came from pretty different worlds. But I enjoyed talking with her. I knew it wasn't really much of anything. But it felt good.

"I should head home," I said.

She acted disappointed. "I'll walk you home."

"Noooo," I said. "Then you'd have to walk home alone in the dark. I'll see you later."

I walked to the door and turned and thanked her. She approached me and gave me a hug. She smelled like cotton candy.

"See ya later," I said.

"Ok. Maybe tomorrow?"

"Maybe, yea."

I stepped into the fresh summer night. My heart was pounding. I jogged most of the way home. When I arrived home dad was on the couch watching TV. He asked me if I had a good time with "the girl?"

I said, "Yea. She's cool."

He asked me if I liked her. I told him it wasn't really like that.

"She likes YOU. Why don't you like her?"

I told him it wasn't really like that.

"I'm going to bed, Dad."

He said goodnight and I went to my room and closed the door and locked it behind me. I put on a record with the volume low and lied down on my water bed. My head was swirling with strange ideas and excitement.

How would my father know if Mia Gray liked me? And why was she being so goddamned friendly? What did she want from me? I had nothing for a girl like that.

My basement room had a large window that looked out onto the carport. I could see past the carport into the night sky. Everything felt so good. I found myself so warm and dizzy and hopeful and I felt like I was real and people were starting to see me as real.

I kicked my shoes off and stripped my tight jeans off. I threw my t-shirt on the floor and I let my head flounder in all the wonderful chemicals that were filling my mind. I had just started to doze and I was awoken by a knock on the door. I lifted my head.

"Yea?"

No one answered.
Another knock startled me. It was coming from the window. My heart bounced around in my chest like a damned basketball.

I focused my sleepy eyes on the glass.
It was Mia Gray.
What did she want?

I squeezed the latch and slid the window open.
The bottom of the window hit her at about her waist.
She had a huge smile on her face.

"Can I come in?" She asked with a mischievous giggle.

God! What was this about? My lower body beneath my sheet was reacting in ways I wasn't prepared for.

She didn't wait for an answer. She leaned in and slid head first through the window.

She landed on top of me and put her mouth to mine. I could taste red wine on her lips. Her hands held my head with her fingers straddling my ears. She kissed me hard. It felt like she meant it. I saw stars. I actually saw stars.

My whole body shuddered and I tried not to let her feel it. She kept her mouth on mine and pulled her shirt off and threw it on the floor with mine.

We kissed hard and eventually slipped under the sheet. We wrapped more affection and passion around each other than I thought I would ever feel. For a moment I worried about my parents hearing us. But then I gave into this singular moment.

My moment.
I fell asleep against Mia Gray's soft, warm body and she fell asleep in my arms.

I was happy.
I could feel my mouth saying so without help from my voice.

She reached into my ribs
And my frame shook.

My benevolent witch
picked her teeth with my bones

And she remembered the taste
of all my sins.

Then she wiped my indiscretion
from her lips

And tossed my ribs into a pile,
where the bellowing frogs
mourned me.

Natural light flooded the hospital room.

I roused from what could only have been dozing.
My left shoulder hurt. I pulled myself up and shaped
myself into a more human figure. It must have been
noon or so. I had slumped down into the hard bedside
chair a little after ten am and almost immediately
dozed off in a terribly uncomfortable position.
It didn't matter. I was exhausted. I needed sleep.

My wife was asleep in the bed next to me. The nurse
had set the bed at an incline so that Kirsten would be
more comfortable.

I arched my back and stretched my arms toward the
ceiling and heard a quiet pop come from my shoulder.
I had that subtle nausea that comes from too little
sleep. My eyes burned and were drawn to the window.
It framed a gray, Arizona winter day.

There were crows collected on the power line across the
street. They leapt into a graceful murder and carried on
about something.

This would be the image that outlasted all others from the day our fourth child was born. Except for the moment Phoebe was cut from Kirsten's belly. The incision and initial gush of blood spilling across her skin were things I'd seen a few times before. Things that would send most people gutted and staggering no longer effected me.

Kirsten's OBGYN had become a dear friend. He was a congenial Jew from our exclusive neighborhood in Scottsdale. He wanted to be handsome. He wore his gray salted curly hair in a longish nineties style and tucked his Polo shirt into pleated and cuffed khaki pants. He had a warm smile and was goddamned genuine.

He visited me for lunch every other week at the restaurant I managed. He was always intrigued by the minutiae of running a large restaurant.

The man cutting my wife open--to forcibly birth our child, was enthralled with busser's schedules and liquor inventories.

I had seen all of our children born in this manner.
Actors in masks and paper costumes on their marks waiting for the protagonist to enter. The theater silent, and brightly lit. The happy Jew queued in the wings.

Then all at once it begins.
In the way that the first dramatic note bursts from the pit and startles you, the actors begin a seemingly violent pageant. It felt wrong for a child to be part of this scene.

The orchestra swells. A broad furrow is cut to make way for the new character. Blood pours over stainless and towels and hurried hands. Then at once, a quiet blue face appears under the hot lights.

There was a new star.

Phoebe's voice filled the room. It rose like a hymn and broke my heart and then mended it. And she would break it again many times.

I stood over the scene. A solitary audience. My wife lay prostrate on the table, in and out of consciousness. Phoebe and I saw each other. We didn't just notice one another. Newborns initially only see bursts of light and shadows. But, I'm certain Phoebe saw my whole soul during her first moments in that sterile and cold room. So we both wept and we saw each other.

Our other three children, Maggie, Shelby, and Emerson had all been born with olive complexions and dark hair--clear products of Kirsten and me. Phoebe showed up as a ginger. Light, almost reddish hair and light eyes. She looked like Kirsten's father.

George was a short round man. Terribly rich. Kind and generous to those with whom he agreed. Cold, arrogant, and ugly with those he didn't. I rather liked him when Kirsten and I first married. He bought me expensive gifts and took me shopping for Italian shoes and suits. Because of him, we drove new luxury cars every year. He helped us buy our first home and took us on regular trips.

He assumed the role of mentor to me as I had come from a poor family and to him that meant my father was a failure.

It didn't take long for me to figure out he was just grateful someone wanted to be with his daughter. Emotionally, it meant less work for him. It meant he could breath.

Now his daughter would have someone else to drive her to the psychiatrist's office. He could get some rest now that she had someone new to be the object of her wrath. Up to that point, everything was his fault.

Now all of her struggles and irrational misery belonged to me.

That was worth all the money in the world to George.

At first my pride wouldn't allow me to graciously accept his gifts and money. I slowly grew into it. Just before Kirsten and I married, George took me to lunch at an embarrassingly posh French bistro at the prestigious Biltmore Plaza on Camelback road. The service staff were sharp and seemed to fear all of their clients.

They served bread and butter with the seriousness of funeral directors. George had other business so lunch was brief. He informed me, as if it were good news, that by marrying his daughter I would not be eligible for educational grants, and loans wouldn't be necessary.

Additionally, if we were to have children while I was in school, the medical costs would be covered. He had accumulated his wealth primarily through his sales skills. Eventually, I decided all of this was an acceptable arrangement. It was payment for services rendered. I was on the payroll now. I earned every goddamned penny he gave me.

Later that afternoon, Kirsten's family began arriving. Her mother, Jocelyn, corralled our other three kids in the small, private hospital room. She had kept them overnight. She could see I was worn thin. She was mostly considerate of me and I often felt that she knew

I had been drafted into the family and that I was being carefully managed.

My family lived far away. I called my parents shortly after Phoebe was born to give them the news. The conversation was short and they offered their well wishes and my mother cried.

The kids cooed over Phoebe and Kirsten spoke in slow monotones between soft scowls as she worked through the pain. There were many things I didn't like about Kirsten. But I admired her durability. She had done this a few times before. Voluntarily. It was her duty as wife and as a "Daughter of God." Our Mormon parents and peers expected it. And we were too young and too well indoctrinated to know any better.

The weeks and months passed. Kirsten and I did exactly what we were supposed to do. No one can tell me otherwise. She kept a goddamned clean house and prepared our four kids organic feed.

I worked 70 hours a week opening restaurants and providing a respectable living for my family.

It was hard work, but I enjoyed it. At work, I was surrounded by people who admired me. Many of them were young, attractive girls who paid me a good deal of attention. To them I was safe. I had four young children. I was happily married.
It was a lie.

I began to use it to my advantage. Not for some perverted purpose. It was part of a slow and steady building of my ego. I sought out situations in which my ego could be carefully cultivated.
It would serve me well later in my life.

Some of the girls would come to me with questions about their college courses or a challenge in their literature class.
Some would ask for a private conversation in the office and once the door closed they would confide in me a problem they were having with a boyfriend.

I was warm water to them. They could slowly slip into me without fear of chill or scald.

My assistant manager was a single man. He was in his late thirties, but acted like a drunk frat boy all the time. He was beyond arrogant, sexist, condescending, and full of machismo. Sexual harassment was still a fringe concept in the industry, so his advances were mostly met with rolled eyes and discomfort.
He didn't have a chance.

These weren't West Hollywood Euro trash girls. These were white bread girls in their freshman years studying economics at Maricopa Community College.
He was cold water. I was their evening bath.

So I capitalized on this, not by taking advantage of these girls, but by allowing their attention to fuel my ego.

My wife would come to work for lunch and bring the kids. After they finished their lunch, I would help her to our embarrassing SUV, strap the kids in and then say goodbye to her. There was never a public display of affection or anything overtly emotional. We usually hugged briefly with a quick, flat-handed pat on the back.

When I returned from the parking lot to the restaurant, I'd notice a few of the girls looking at me with fucking puppy dog eyes. They'd go on about their business. Standing in front of computer terminals, closing checks, checking their phones, averting their eyes when I looked at them.

The minute I entered the dining room, I'd go into professional mode. I'd look for shit on the floor and ask a busser to clean it up. I'd count how many servers were still on the clock and consult with the hostess about cutting staff.

Then I'd make my way to the office in the back of the kitchen. Along the way one of the servers would walk beside me and tell me how much she admired my dedication to my family.

I would tell her my wife "...Is a goddess."

It was a lie. In the same way that my father lied, I lied. I was saying what my father said about his wife. I was making myself seem emotionally powerful by suggesting that I worshiped the woman I decided to marry.

It wasn't a compliment to her. It wasn't designed to build her up and frighten off the competition. I said it because it made me look good. It took me a few years to realize this. The only thought that makes me feel less stupid is that every man does this in varying degrees.

Every man lacks something at home. He either makes up for it in his professional life or in his social interactions with others. For the average married heterosexual male, interactions with other women are the only measure of his worth. We live in a patriarchal culture where men are considered the dominant sex.

The reality of this pathetic order is that women are, without question, the more powerful of the sexes.

This idea may not be reflected in gender economy or within the social construct where women wait for men to tell them what to do. But, for honest men who have learned to properly diagnose their illness, women aren't just holding all the cards, they're wearing a goddamned royal flush across all of their sultry curves while masking their intellects with aces. Men who have nothing more than a penis and lay down their hand deserve to be laughed at by the dealer.

So I played my hand, and I played it often.

My wife would call me late at night while I was closing down the restaurant. She would ask me why I wasn't home yet.

"It's 2:30 in the morning! You closed at midnight! Why aren't you home? Is there someone there with you?" She was always so damned suspicious. Most of the time I was counting money and reconciling invoices.

Sometimes, I was playing cards.

So, we played our hands. We played hand after hand for years. The game was always the same. I opened and ran restaurants where there were attractive people who enjoyed what I had to offer.

She effectively managed our children and all things household. During those years, we built a handful of custom homes. She worked closely with architects, interior designers, and landscapers to ensure we had a beautiful place in which to live.

In the in between we fought like pound dogs and scratched out our wants and needs with sticks in cement.

We could never seem to understand each other.

I thought I was so simple and I could never understand her emotional outbursts.
She thought I was so simple and she could never understand her emotional outbursts.

Kirsten and I had just built a house in an up-and-coming neighborhood in the McDowell Mountain Ranch area of Scottsdale, Arizona. The house was an unnecessarily large place with lots of slate tile and berber carpeting. I had the three car garage floor painted and sealed because my father-in-law told me it was important to be able to keep your garage floor clean. I had contractors install a special wall for hanging tools. I didn't have any tools, really. So, I bought enough tools to fill the new wall.

I screwed large industrial hooks into the ceiling of the garage for the kids bikes. The kids were too small to hang their own bikes and I was never home, so the bikes littered the drive and garage.

Kirsten wanted us to have a uniquely landscaped yard, so we hired her father's landscaper. He was a talented and shrewd yardman.

The evening my father-in-law referred him to me, we were having an early dinner at Houston's, a pricier and prettier version of TGIF's. He and Jocelyn picked us up in their new Lexus sedan. After months of research, Kirsten and I had found a babysitter capable of managing our litter for a couple of hours.

We were greeted at the front door by a stunning woman who was designated the hostess of this lousy little meat slinging "Bistro."

This was the New World Order for the Nouveau Riche. They left London and Paris and Milano and bought condos in Napa and Scottsdale.

Napa held fast to its roots and served foie gras and muddy pinot noirs.

Scottsdale forged new gods.
Dry and dirty desert gods who wanted posher meat.

They had a grittier vision of food and fantasy. These people were two generations earlier and smarter than our current hipster culture.

Unlike our current Northwestern hipster cult, Scottsdale was a, "Fuck you! I'm going to wear a tight black dress and my date is going to wear some blue Sinatra slacks and we're going to do a couple of fat lines on a table in a closed section near the emergency exit in the back of a Denny's."

"Why would you do this! I'm your fucking wife! What about your four fucking children! Life is so easy for you, isn't it!"

I pulled my 1990 silver Volvo into the garage. Once the hanging tennis ball was touching my windshield, put it in park and turned the engine off.

I pressed the button on the remote and the door rolled down behind me. Whenever I came home this late, I worried the garage door motor would wake Kirsten. Our house was well built and the master bedroom was situated in the back of the house. Normally, it wasn't the garage door that would wake her.
It was me crawling into bed.

I sat for a moment while the engine creaked and cooled. The light on the garage door motor flashed, letting me know it would soon go off. I didn't care. Exhaustion and anxiousness were battling for my attention.
Anyway, I knew my way through the garage in the dark. I'd traveled that path a hundred times.

We didn't keep liquor in the house. Shit.

I had plenty of whiskey in my blood to keep me warm and happy for another hour or two.

I would slip through the door leading into the mud room where I would listen for the alarm queue. I was certain that Kirsten would sometimes set the alarm so that I would be bothered and so she could hear me come in. Tonight she hadn't. I kicked my loafers off. Then I made my way down the hallway, through the family room to the sliding glass door.

I quietly slid it closed behind me.

When I got to the pool deck, I began peeling my clothes off. The deck was still warm from the desert sun.

I walked naked toward the deep end, sat down on the edge, placed my palms on the deck, stiffened my arms, and slipped--without a splash--into the water. My feet were sore, my head was hot, and I was a little drunk.

I felt like I could just keep sinking into the clear, cool, velvety wet. I fought the urge to paddle or swim.
I allowed myself to sink to the bottom.

When my sore feet lit on the bottom of the pool, I opened my eyes and looked up through the clear water into the bright night sky.

It was always a dream.

My life had become a church fire. An event filled with heat and wailing and blame, peppered with some pretty music now and then.

This was my pretty music.

I planted both feet on the concrete at the bottom of the pool and pushed myself to the surface. I filled my lungs with the cool dry weight of the desert. I could taste saguaro and sage and prickly pear. The burn of chlorine in my throat washed down the stinging diesel from an earlier bump of cocaine I had done right before leaving the restaurant.

I bounced up and down and toyed with my weightlessness as though it was something that I had created. As if it were mine.

The arrogance with which boys do this dance is an embarrassment. Smooth skinned, white boys wiping the water from their eyes and spitting across the surface of the pool is a flat out farce. The way they spring off of their toes and broadcast their buoyancy is something akin to a goddamned barnyard peacock. As if the water were their toy. As if they had some unique power over the greatest of elements.
Perhaps it's because we're stronger in water.

As men, we've been taught, our whole lives, to be stronger. To be more manly. To stand up taller. To push, to pull harder. To not cry. To not act like a girl. To run faster. To demand more from our women. And if they don't satisfy our demands, to take control of them. As men, our poolside manner is just another practice for the prom.

"What the hell are you doing?"

I turned toward the scowling voice.

It was Kirsten. She was standing above me in her bare feet and expensive silk pajamas on the house side of the pool deck.

I knew this drill. I responded flatly, "I'm unwinding."

"Unwinding from what? You run a fucking restaurant, you're not the damned prime minister of Russia!" She was yelling the way my father did when I was a small boy. Not with volume, but quite nearly a whisper through closed teeth and narrow lips.

"What's the harm?" I asked. "I'm being quiet. I'm not waking anyone."

"It's just not normal! You're a grown man! You're swimming naked at almost three in the morning! When are you going to grow up!" She spun gracefully on the ball of her left foot and made for the patio door.

Kirsten had been a dancer in her youth and in college. She attended the prestigious Cornish Institute and spoke incessantly of Martha Graham and Mikhail Baryshnikov when we first met. Among her many skills were her physical grace and control. Before we began over-populating the earth, she would often dance for me in the kitchen. It was an absolute wonder to watch her move. I never joined her. It wasn't that kind of dancing. She was the dancer. I was the clumsy cook.

When she reached the sliding glass door, she repeated the choreography, spun around and said, "If you're not coming to bed right now, just sleep on the couch."

She turned back toward the door, opened it slightly, and slipped through it into the house.

She actually slammed the sliding glass door shut!

That couldn't have been easy. It was a heavy door and she was 5'1" and 100lbs.

Jesus. I disliked sleeping on the couch. I never slept well and my body felt it the entire day after.

I swam to the stairs at the shallow end of the pool.

I climbed the four steps to the deck. I stood naked and dripping and stared up at the stars. I felt my skin raising in the cool air. A sudden shiver snapped me from my star gazing. I was cold. I pulled a towel from off of one of the pool chairs. I pressed it to my face and took a deep breath. I could smell sunscreen in it. One of the kids must have been using it earlier in the day.

I dried off, grabbed all of my clothing in one hand and went inside. The air conditioning was on and it was quite chilly in the house.

I set the alarm and went to the shower in the hallway.

I quickly cleaned the chlorine off of my skin and ran hot water over my face and in my mouth. The last thing I needed was for Kirsten to smell whiskey on my face or in my breath. The smell of China would go right over her head. But the smell of whiskey was trap. A damned sad deal breaker.

I quickly dried off, brushed my teeth, turned off the light, and went to our bedroom. I pulled the covers back and slipped cautiously into the sheets. They were clean smelling and the fragrance of conditioner coming from my wife's hair was inviting. I pulled sheet and comforter up over my shoulders.

Kirsten had her back to me. I slowly moved my cold feet toward hers until our toes touched. Her feet responded ever so slightly.
We lightly caressed legs and feet and toes with the lilt of a priest sprinkling holy water over a grave.

Soon, our feet and legs became hungry and earnest and the caresses were exchanged for grabs and pulls and in the early hours of the morning, we let go of all of the requirements of our broken and burning egos and dug a little deeper into each other. Just enough grace and clumsiness to make more scar tissue. Just enough sadness to pretend it was love.

I've swam this long and dirty pond too
many times.
I'm desperate for a hook.
I'm longing to be laid out on a platter.
My angry devils in this rocking boat,
Keep poking at my swollen scales.

The thing I learned about relationships and marriage at a very early age was that they are hard.

Marriage is a holy union doused in gasoline. The soul objective a married man has is to not light a match. Nothing about marriage is pleasurable or smooth. It is a steady struggle and a goddamned grind, at best. When measured against these truths, I had a very good life.

Yes, I was married to a woman who despised me and derided me at every opportunity. Yes, we fought much more than daily. Yes, our fights would often keep us up all night if one of the kids didn't.
Yes, I felt like I was suffocating.

To be fair, however, we had a great sex life. We had four perfectly lovely children. We had a nice home in a gated community. We drove nice cars.

Well... Kirsten drove nice cars. I drove my old Volvo.

We traveled when and where we liked. I was moving rapidly through the ranks with my company--likely, the direct result of me spending so much time at work because I hated going home.

I had been promoted recently and was bringing home $70,000 a year in addition to bonuses, medical insurance, company matched 401k, and $400 in free food a month at the restaurant I managed.
We also got a monthly stipend of $2,000-$5,000 from Kirsten's father, depending on our particular needs and expenses that month.

Based upon every standard I'd been taught, we had a damned good life.

If I ever became upset with Kirsten's behavior or if she ever struck me with a magazine or a book while I was sleeping, I would steam about it for a while, but in the end, I would reason with myself.

"Look, Charles. You have a good life. This is how marriages are. You saw your parents go through similar tribulations. This is how it works. No matter who you were married to, it would be the same."

We didn't have any close friends, as anytime we began developing friendships with other couples Kirsten would assume I was inappropriately interested in the other wife and a fight would ensue.

Or sometimes after a couple had gone home from an evening of dinner and cards, she would demand to know why I seemed ashamed of my occupation. Why I talked like I should've chosen another career path.

"Don't you DARE hang this on me, you asshole! I didn't force you to go to Chef school! You're a fucking GROWN MAN! You made that decision of your own accord. Now you have to grow up and own your decisions! There's no going back now! You're in it!"

Sometimes she would take issue with the way I loaded the dishwasher. Not in a quietly irritated way. But in a "You better loosen your tie, this is going to take all night" sort of irritated way.

I looked at other couples and I could see challenges and missteps in their social dynamics. I could see all the little hiccups that would lead to them going home and fighting all night.

Surely they were not far different from us.
This was marriage. This was simply what being married was all about.

Right?

I heard Carly Simon coming from the bathroom before I even knew what day it was. This goddamned song was Kirsten's anthem. It was her feeble attempt to express her power as a woman. She often played it in the early mornings when I was trying to sleep.

She only required a few hours of sleep a night.
She wasn't human. She knew it. She rubbed it in as frequently as she liked.

We could stay up until five in the morning fighting and she would be up without an alarm at six-thirty, cleaning the grout between the kitchen tiles and shining our commercial grade stainless steel appliances.

My face was buried in the down pillow. The sweet smell of laundry detergent swirled around my aching head.

Our bedroom was quite large. Twenty feet away was a sliding door that lead to the side of the house where there was an outdoor shower. Kirsten had opened the long, red velvet drapes and the spring sunshine was blazing through the glass. The window faced north so we weren't getting direct sunlight but it was Arizona. There was sunshine everywhere. It was a miserable irritation to me. We ran the air conditioning 24/7 from April to November.

It was Saturday. I could hear the kids engaged in activities that didn't involve hurried dressing and orders being barked by Carly fucking Simon.

I sat up on the edge of the bed, facing the large, opened French doors of our bedroom.

Emerson came bursting into the bedroom crying or laughing or something.
It was just a great deal of ... loud.
He was four years old and was just an amalgam of bones and dirt and noise and peanut butter.

He didn't notice me sitting there and ran right into the bathroom to tell his mother something awful and traumatic. Phoebe was right behind him. She was three and had snow white, curly hair. She was pure happiness.

Even when she was upset and crying about something, I could make her laugh and completely forget about the injury or offense. She followed Emerson's trajectory into the bathroom but, she noticed me sitting there. She stopped and looked at me.

"Daaaaaaad!"

She ran to me and jumped up on my lap. She was wearing a floral Gap dress. Her hair was a curly disaster.

Kirsten did the older girls' hair everyday. For whatever reason, she allowed Phoebe's hair to just be.

Phoebe's hair was reminiscent of my cats claw locks from the seventies.

This child was one of only a few things that kept me tethered to this sweltering Arizona mortality. I adored her with my whole soul.

I pulled her close and she leaned her sweaty little head into my bare chest. I kissed her hot head and ran my hands across her rat's nest and over her round face in the same way my father did.

In that moment, the smell of my father's hands filled the room with olfactory memories. I wondered if she would remember the smell of my hands and the way I stroked her hair. I wanted her to have fond and hopeful memories. I wanted her to write about the smell of my hands and the comfort of being held by me.

She rambled on about something Emerson had done and a toy and a marker and her bike being broken.
I was in boxers.

Kirsten came out of the bathroom pulling Emerson by the hand. "Don't you think you should put some clothes on?"

I looked at my bare legs and chest.

"It's a little inappropriate for you to be holding your daughter like that, don't you think?"

I kissed Phoebe on the crown of her head, stood up and tossed her on the bed. She landed on her back and broke into laughter.

"Agaaaaaain, Daddddddd!"

She held her arms toward me, waiting for me to pick her up.

Emerson broke away from his mother and ran to me. He wrapped his arms around my legs.

"Me, Daddd!!!! Throw meee!!"

I picked Emerson up and threw him in the air. Our ceilings were twelve-foot ceilings. Plenty of room for small, flying humans.

I tossed him on the bed next to Phoebe. They slapped at each other and giggled and demanded more.

"Nooooo. I can't stand you smelly kids! I have to put clothes on!"

Emerson protested. "No clothessss! No clothes!"

Phoebe had to compete.
"Daddddd! One more throw meee!"

"Your mom says I need clothes on."

I looked at her like I had cornered her King.
She looked at me like she had cornered my Queen.

"Your Dad shouldn't be walking around without clothes on. That's gross, isn't it, kidsss?"

Emerson and Phoebe echoed her sentiment.

"Ewwww. Grosssss!" Phoebe swatted her hand in front of her face. Emerson laughed and plugged his nose.

I headed toward the bathroom and looked over my shoulder, sticking my tongue out at them. They laughed and howled and their mother ordered them to the kitchen.

"I have to leave in less than 30 minutes. Can you get it together so that I can depend on you to handle the kids?"

She closed the French doors behind her.

Jesus H. Christ! Can you FUCK off already.

I turned on the shower and buried my sleeplessness in hot water. Kirsten left the music in the bathroom on. It was the Cranberries now. So much good music spoiled by sour memories.

I loved Saturdays.

Wait... I hated every day.
Let me start over.

Saturdays were the best day of my week. I had the whole day with the kids. I had worked my way up the corporate ladder and now had weekends off.

Sunday was filled with religious practice and country club misery.

Saturday was usually the day that Kirsten spent the day shopping and lunching and gossiping and privileging with her mother.

I turned off the shower, squeegeed the glass door, got out and dried off and went into the closet to find something to wear.

I have never been a normal man as it relates to attire. I have never been a jeans and t-shirt kind of man.

I disliked the Arizona climate. Who, in their right mind, would live in a place where spontaneous combustion was a common occurrence? Where was the pleasure in living in such a God-forsaken, burning dust bowl?

I found some light plaid pants and a long sleeve, linen shirt. I slipped some brown leather sandals on and wandered to the front of the house.

When I came out of the hallway and into the family room, all the kids were sitting at the kitchen table. It was an eight foot long, roughly hewn pine table with a long wooden bench down one side. Shelby saw me and ran toward me and jumped into my arms.

Shelby was five years old. She has always been fussy and temperamental. Her first eighteen months were a blur. Night after night of colic and crying and sleepless night after sleepless night. She only found comfort in me.

She would lose her shit over something one of the other kids had done or her stomach would hurt or she would be tired and fussy and she would always come straight to me. If her mother or her grandmother were holding her during one of these episodes, they would hand her off to me.

To this day I don't understand what it was. But I was the soft sway that Shelby wanted when her world spun too fast.

I picked her up and squeezed her. She lay her head under my chin.

"Daddd. Can I have a pop sickle?"

"Shelby, it's breakfast time. Have you had some breakfast?"

"Can't I have a pop sickle for breakfast?" She whined.

"Of course you can't, you crazy kid."

"I'm not crazy."

Kirsten was all business. She had her hands in running water, washing god knows what.

"Can you please fix the third garage door today? There's something wrong with the sensor."

I tried to be decent. "Yea. I'll take care of it."

"Thank you."
She seemed to be trying to be decent as well.

She told the kids she was leaving and began kissing foreheads and cheeks.

Maggie got fussy.

"I want to go with you and grandma."

Kirsten reasoned with her. "Grandma and I have to talk about Easter stuff."

The kids became all excited and electrified by the idea of Easter. They laughed and ooh'd and aah'd. Kirsten gave Maggie an extra long hug and then headed toward the garage door.

I heard the door slam and the garage door motor hum. I only had to wait for the magical sound of the garage door closing and my whole world began to expand and contract in such a beautiful rhythm that it was as if the universe were lying down in deep green grass on a clear summer day.

The kids finished their granolas and their yogurts and their cucumber and provolone quesadillas and their steel cut oats with soy milk and I sent them to play in the back yard while I cleaned up the evidence of their consumption.

After I cleaned the table and swept underneath it and washed all of the kid-slop hardware and set it to dry, I went out and sat in one of our Home Depot chaise lounge chairs with a can of organic cream soda and took a few deep breaths and listened to the sweet sound of my children laughing and playing in the sand and dirt and cactus needles.

Later, I yelled at them to come inside. They didn't like that idea, so I told them I'd play guitar and we could sing songs. That was the candy-sweet cattle call needed to bring all of my perfect offspring running. In a matter of moments, all of my Old Navy covered spawn were gathered around me and begging for a few Blue's Clues chords.

It only took one strum to bring smiles to all of their round, sweaty faces.

Music changes all of us.
Every goddamned citizen of planet Earth has at least one beautiful memory associated with music. One chord has the power to raise Lazarus from his lazy nap.

I was never a musician. But I've always enjoyed making noise. Music. Words. Car horns.

We dance to music. We fall asleep to it. We drink with it. We play it in our cars. We worship our useless gods to it. We fuck to it. We bury our lovers to it. For God's sake, we buy and sell music. And since it's not a textile, it must be a goddamned drug.

I was a small time drug dealer. And these littles were my schoolyard clients.

I played lots of E's and made up words.

"Ohhhhhh... Phoebe is a sandy little cactus girl. With bits of cactus in ev-er-y curl. She's sweeter and quicker than a standard squirrel."

"Dadddd! Sing a song about me!" Emerson insisted.

"Ohhhhh... Emerson likes to make lots of noise. And rarely puts away his toys. He's probably the reason we had no more boys."

"Dadddd!"

Emerson whined. He didn't like my song.
The girls cackled like old southern quilting ladies. I played all the same notes in different combinations for more than an hour. The kids laughed and cried and danced and tumbled and poked at each other and my fingers hurt.

The rest of the afternoon was standard part-time father fare. The kids watched videos in their playroom while I accidentally found porn and searched for car deals on my big box Mac. I was three cream sodas deep and anything could happen.

I backed the Volvo out of the garage and wiped the few oil spots off of the lacquered concrete.

I changed the timer on the sprinkler system in the front yard to accommodate the coming summer heat.

I swept the expensive rocks that we used as ground cover off the aggregate concrete trail in the backyard-- Emerson's handy work. He was a boy to the bone.

Always throwing rocks. Constantly haranguing his sisters. Frequently losing his pants. New bruises and scrapes and cuts and bad words every day--probably my fault.

Or those shitty kids at church.

Carefully woven into his gritty, boyish fabric was a sweet and sensitive soul that made me believe that one day he might change the world.

Or at the very least he would seduce the whole of female humanity. And that would make me proud.

I cleaned the pool filters and skimmed the water with the net. We had a pool boy, but this is what white country club folk did. We paid a Mexican to purify our swimming water and when we were bored with our shitty white privileged lives, we lifted a long aluminum pole with a fine net at the end and trapped a few rogue blossoms and griped about our cluttered lives. It made us feel valuable and complex. It made us feel less uncomfortable in our thin, entitled skin.

Around six o'clock I heard the garage door open.
I quickly powered down the Mac and slipped into the kid's playroom. I sat on the futon couch and feigned interest in the program they were watching.

They were mostly spent. Phoebe was sucking her thumb and twirling her hoary locks. Emerson was lying on his stomach on the floor, slowly kicking his feet on the carpet. Shelby had sunk deep into the sofa, motionless and doe-eyed with her dark, deep set eyes. Maggie heard the garage door and jumped up to go greet her mother. She ran down the hall and through the laundry room and opened the door.

"Maggie! Don't go out there until your mom turns the car off!"

"I won't, Dad!"

The engine shut down. Car doors opened and closed and opened and closed again. Bags rustled.

"Mommmm! Why were you gone so long?"

Maggie was attached to her mom. She disregarded me from a young age. She was my first born and I loved her deeply. But she was old when she was young, and she began managing me early on. She didn't trust me and I trusted her even less. When she became an adult, that dynamic gained traction and we would always be at odds with one another.

There was a good deal of noise as Kirsten and Maggie wrestled with bags through the laundry room and into the hallway. I would have helped, but it was important that Kirsten saw me sitting in the playroom with the kids. It would fortify my position as a good father. In and of itself, it wouldn't make for a strong case. But on a long enough timeline, the regular sight of me bored, and sitting with the kids would surely confirm my character as a father and caretaker.

They continued through the hall and went past the playroom without stopping. They went straight into the kitchen. I heard bags being set on the floor and Maggie questioning her mother.

"Why were you gone so long? Where did you go? Ohhhhh! What's this? Where's grandma? Did you guys go out to eat? When's Easter? What are we having for dinner?"

Jesus. Did the child ever breathe?

I held firmly to my post. My reputation was at stake. I pulled Phoebe closer and kept my arm around her.

"CHARLESSSS???"

Kirsten called from the kitchen.

I pretended not to hear her. Phoebe looked up at me. I looked down at her. We didn't say anything, but we understood each other. Phoebe would always be an ally.

The TV remote was on the sofa within reach. I grabbed it and turned up the volume on the television. The kids loved the Big Rock Candy Mountain song. It was a treat for them to hear it loud.

"CHARLESSSS! CAN YOU COME IN HERE?"

I turned the volume up three or four more bars. If I had developed any strength in my marriage with Kirsten, it was a keen stubbornness. I had staying power.

I heard Kirsten's graceful feet tapping across the tile toward the playroom.
Mission accomplished.

She appeared in the doorway.
Her petite frame was frightening.

"Could you not hear me calling you?"

"Oh. Wait... Were you calling me?"

My face was plastered with surprise and apology.
"Sorry, Honey. I guess the TV was up too loud. Let me turn it down."

I pointed the remote at the TV screen and adamantly pressed the volume button.

Phoebe looked up at me again. She was the wisest damned person in the room.

"Haven't you started dinner yet?"

She was literally just in the kitchen. She was a hawk, this woman. If there was a single pot out of place or if the kitchen temperature rose above seventy-six degrees Fahrenheit due to a gas flame, she would have immediately noticed. The question was so goddamned rhetorical, even Phoebe looked up at me again.

"No. I wasn't sure if you wanted to do take-out or what?"

Kirsten stared at me and she was so disappointed, I was forced to be the next one to use words.

"I wasn't sure how late you'd be. I didn't want to make dinner and have it get cold."

She was still looking at me with her mouth closed. She clearly had no intention of saying anything. She folded her arms and leaned a shoulder against the door frame.

Fuck.

Fuck. Fuck. Fuck.

She was a fucking magician. She could take an ordinary moment and turn it into a catastrophe that rivaled the Holocaust.

I still had my arm around Phoebe and I'm certain she could feel my blood pressure rise.

She looked up at me again.

"How bout we order take-out from the restaurant? Me and Phoebes and Emerson will go pick it up."

"I want to goooo!" Shelby cried.

"Yes! You can go too," I replied.

Kirsten softened her posture and said, "Ok. Do you still have money left on your company card?"

"Well," I said, "I wouldn't order if I didn't."

I knew how to be shitty too.

She turned and walked away. Phoebe looked up at me. I looked at her and we understood each other. We had won the battle. But the war was just loosening its belt to prepare for the feast.

That summer, Phoebe broke her arm.

Kirsten had decided she felt unimportant and that she might want more stimulation in her life, so she enrolled in a couple of classes at Scottsdale Community College.

One of the benefits was discounted child care. We were always opposed to childcare. Unless it was a person we had carefully screened and who came to our home, we didn't leave our kids with anyone.

But we were a nuclear family. We were evolving and becoming part of a forward thinking culture. You had to leave your kids with people if you wanted to accomplish things. But you had to be careful not to let on that it was for your own selfish purposes. You had to formulate a mantra that convinced people that you were doing what was best for your children.

"Yeaaa... I chose Scottsdale Community College's Youth Development Program because their curriculum really focuses on early socialization and they don't allow parents to bring any peanut products or foods with artificial dyes in their kids lunches."

The fuck we did. At that time, in my parental intellect, I couldn't give more than two shits whether or not my kids were exposed to peanut butter or red dye 40. We left our fucking kids with complete strangers because they belonged to an organization we assumed had their best interests in mind.

So that's what we did.

I got in my Volvo every morning and drove to work. Kirsten piled the four kids into her luxury whip, dropped one off at Montessori where she kissed her on the forehead and sent her off to be properly conditioned and then drove to her exciting, new learning institution where she parked on a large, hot tarmac and walked the other three kids to the peanut-free annex. Once they were seemingly safe, she headed off to class.

On one of those days I was in my office wrestling with an accounts receivable issue when the phone rang.

I knew Daniella, the hostess, would get it. The line was put on hold and flashed red. The intercom beeped and Daniella's voice came from the speaker.

"Charles?"

"Yes, Daniella?"

"Your wife is on line one."

"Thank you, Daniella."

"De nada, Carlos."

Daniella was a pretty faced Latina girl who had become my most trusted staff member. She could run the store as well as I could. The best thing the company could ever have done would have been to fire me and give her my job. They could have paid her $30,000 less a year and they would've gotten someone with twice the work ethic.

She was curvy and flirty and we had a playful and comfortable working relationship. One night in the first few months that we worked together, she met me in the back of the kitchen near the office and asked me if I wanted to see her tattoo. Not many girls in Scottsdale had tattoos in the nineties.
OF COURSE I wanted to see her tattoo.

She turned her back to me, leaned over a prep table, arched her back, stuck her ass out in an unnecessarily dramatic and sensual fashion and lifted her blouse to reveal a small, shitty tribal blotch of ink in the small of her back.

She asked me if I wanted to touch it. I did want to.
But I didn't. I was loyal to my wife. She was the mother of my children. She was a "Goddess" as I often told the girls with whom I worked.

Touching a curvy Latina girl's bare skin on the small of her back would, most certainly, constitute adultery of some form. I was many things, but I was not a cheater.

I told Daniella to put her shirt down. She obeyed.
She turned around to face me. Pout was pouring from her lips.

"Maybe later," she said.

"Maybe," I said.

What was I talking about! There wasn't going to be any touching now or later or any other time.

I pressed the blinking button and put the receiver to my ear. Kirsten was calling from the emergency room at a hospital in Scottsdale. Phoebe had broken her arm. Apparently, there was a tussle over a bicycle during recess and she fell and broke her radius or ulna. Or both. I don't know. Kirsten was so emotional I was having difficulty understanding the injury.

Phoebe was safe and that's all that mattered.

I parked my silver Volvo wagon between a new white Mercedes and a new white Mercedes in the emergency room parking lot. I walked quickly across the blistering pavement. I was wearing Italian loafers with thin leather soles. The heat was quite uncomfortable on my feet. I took advantage of my long legs and made haste toward the broad automatic sliding doors to the emergency room.

The doors opened and cold air rushed out. Everything in Phoenix was air conditioned. In many instances, uncomfortably so. This was one of those instances.

I had been in many a hospital waiting room in Phoenix. They were notoriously cold. This one was no different. The initial feeling of cold air across my hot face was relieving. However, it quickly became a bit numbing. By the time I inquired at the front desk and found Phoebe and Kirsten, my nose was running.

I used my whole arm to open the blue drape that kept the chaotic flurry of people and equipment and cries and urgent voices separate from Phoebe and her mother.

Phoebe looked up at me from the hospital bed.

I immediately remembered how my heart broke the moment she arrived in this world, when I could see all of the most perfect and frightening moments that lay ahead for her.

Perhaps it's just the way my scattered and broken mind works. She was born and I saw so much beauty and brilliance in her, but immediately saw all of the darkest and most painful possibilities.

As a child, I fell into a state of depression on Christmas morning before any gifts were opened. I knew it would all be over soon and I couldn't bear the finality of the holiday. It was as if I knew Christ belonged to one day and his brother, Lucifer kept watch on all the others. Once gifts were given, the Holy Ghost removed itself from us and quiet hopelessness returned. I always saw the darkness in the tunnel. Never the light at the end.

Phoebe's eyes were filled with tears but they were dull. She wasn't really crying anymore. She shuddered here and there in little after-sobs and memory tremors.

She had an industrial medical blanket over her legs. Her left arm was in a temporary sling. She looked at me as if she needed instructions. She seemed as though she wanted to know if this was ok or if she should dig deep for strength. Or hope. Or help. Or... God.

I looked at Kirsten sitting in the hard, plastic chair next to Phoebe's bed. She had her short legs crossed and the rest of her melted over her thighs and knees.

She looked at me briefly and returned to her messy posture. Everything about her suggested this was on me. She wasn't invested in this project.

I pulled the drape on its track until the gap was closed and I was sure Phoebe couldn't see anything going on outside her sterile, paper shelter.

I took one long, clumsy step around Kirsten's sloppy frame and sat on the bed next to Phoebe. She flinched imperceptibly. She was protecting her wounded arm. My heart sunk further into the empty recesses of my dirty gut. Here and now, Phoebe wasn't my helpless, little, fair haired treasure. She was so human in this moment.

Like an animal adapting to her surroundings. She was like a rose bush. So soft and fragrant and beautiful and iconic and full of thorns and hard roots. She was everything that was wondrous and gorgeous and fragile but she was holding fast to all of the things that would protect her from damage and pain.

I put both of my hands over her hot head. I leaned in and kissed her on her wet forehead.

"We're going home soon."

She shuddered and the corners of her mouth pulled her lips into relief and pouring sadness.

She let go and sobbed against my cheek.

"Everything's going to be fine, Blondie. I love you. We'll be done here soon."

Just then, the thin curtain rings raced across the track and a young intern abruptly entered the bed space.

"Dr. Sterling will be in shortly. Is she comfortable?"

I looked at Kirsten and remembered I was on duty.

"She seems disoriented. Can you explain to me her injury and what we're waiting for?"

"Of course. Are you the father?"

No. I'm the fucking gardener!
YES, I'm the fucking father!

"Yes, Phoebe's my daughter."

"Ok. So... Phoebe has sustained a compound fracture. She's probably experiencing a bit of shock. Dr. Sterling is recommending she be admitted and scheduled for surgery as soon as possible."

"Surgery?" I said. "For what?"

"Well," the kid replied, "She's going to need a couple of pins put in her arm."

The whole dialogue lost its actual verbal structure and landed in my chest, where it began to ache and press on my bones and the details of the diagnosis became secondary to my daughter's immediate relief.

"Can you give her something for the pain?" I asked.

"We've been waiting for Dr. Sterling to give us the green light on some pain medication. I'll check with him again right now."

He was all business. No emotion.
Kirsten was all emotion and absolutely no business.
I had to find footing somewhere in between.

"Imagine you've experienced a compound fracture in your arm and you've been sitting in an ice cold room for nearly two hours. See if that doesn't get you to prescribe some pain medication for my daughter just a smidgen faster."

My face was hot. The clean cut intern smiled nervously and said, "I'll talk with Dr. Sterling immediately."

I sat back down on the edge of Phoebe's bed. I held her good hand and stroked the sweaty, blonde locks off of her forehead. I kissed her head a few times and asked her if she wanted pizza for dinner. She nodded her head and I could tell she wanted to smile. Instead, her small frame sunk and my heart followed. She was folding under the pain.

She made me think of a dandelion bobbing its head in the wind, looking spry and happy enough, and then as the gusts become stronger, the pretty little florets give in and lose their hold and become subject to the will of the wind. All of her exposed nerve endings were losing their wrestle with the wind. Piece by piece they were buckling and falling into a tearful and trembling current.

Phoebe was wheeled into surgery about two hours later. Dr. Sterling put two teflon pins in her arm, they cast her arm and we took her home the next afternoon.

Kirsten was unable to adjust her two community college courses to stay home and care for Phoebe. So I took a leave of absence and some vacation time and stayed home with her for a little over two weeks.

By then, I'd be able to find a girl to come over and sit with her for a few hours a day. The days were filled with reading books, watching movies, careful baths, and drawing pictures on her cast.

When the time finally came to have the pins removed from her elbow, it was scheduled at the doctor's office. The nurse said it would be a quick and painless procedure. Dr. Sterling cut off her cast, cleaned up her arm, and took a pair of medical pliers in hand.

He struggled to remove the first pin as Phoebe screamed in pain. I held her tightly and she buried her face in my shirt. Emerson had come along as he wanted to watch. His face became white as the doctor finally pulled the first pin loose and a thin stream of blood shot from the small hole left by the "Non-stick" pin.

I encouraged my daughter.
"See! One down. The next one will be easier."

Why do we lie to our children? We try so hard to comfort them and we most often use lies to do it. When they ask if the needle will hurt, we say, "Nooooo... you'll barely feel it."

When they ask if the water's cold, we say, "It's not that bad. You'll get used to it."

When they say they don't want to eat their carrots we say, "They're sweet like candy."

When we're 150 miles from our destination, we tell them we're almost there.

150 MILES!

I suspect Moses told the children of Israel the same thing in those forty years of wandering in the desert. I imagine he and his brother, Aaron told the Israelites a few lies to get them to step into the Red Sea. Perhaps lies that foster hope are better than truth that crushes it. Or could it be that we lie because our tongues are trapped behind our teeth and they can't wag, and whisper all the terrible truths that await our progeny if they follow the prophets.

I don't know. I'm not always sure how things work. When times like these arose, I tried remembering what my father did when I was small and powerless. I tried remembering his words so that I could tell my Phoebe similar lies.

Life had changed for me.

Court orders and attorney's fees and notarized emotions and complicated visitation schedules fit across my shoulders and dripped down my arms like a carefully tailored jacket.

One pocket stuffed with cigarettes and bent business cards for discount lawyers.

It was a long winter in the desert.

I'd rather not write about how I arrived at this place. But it's fair. It has to be fair. I cannot write only about the romantic and wistful moments and I cannot only write about hope, a concept I clung to through most of my youth and early adult years.

It's only fair to spell out the quiet times where loss washed over me and where I floundered and eventually drowned. It's only fair that we all feel the weight of water in our throats and lungs.

I want to write with value. And there's value in the few moments where men are holding their own faces and pouring all of their loss into empty rooms, with drafty windows, and slim, rattling doors separating them from the proper parts of life. The parts that were easy and logical. Like busses and drugstores and wind and church marquis and jogging moms and rain and cops and the swinging streetlights at the end of the block.

If I intend to write with value, then I must write about my father telling me he was sick. I mean... I knew he was sick. He'd been sick since I was 13. What I mean is that he called me while I was traveling for work.
I was in my early forties.

"My liver's done."

"Wait. What do you mean your liver's done?"

"I'm on a transplant list."

I had just checked into a Hilton in Salt Lake City.

"I'm here for a couple of days. Want to get a beer?"

There was silence. Nothing. Had he hung up? I held the phone between my shoulder and ear while I hung my starched shirts.

"Dad?"

He had always been in control. I wasn't sure how to lead this dance.

"Yeahhh. Yea, son. Come on over when you're free and we'll talk."

I finished hanging my shirts.

I turned on the television.
I opened the drapes and stared to the west.

Salt Lake City is dreadful in the winter. The view westward does nothing but bury you in gray and icy despair. No wonder the Saints needed Brigham Young to convince them that this was the place.

I met Dad at his condominium in Bountiful--a northern suburb of Salt Lake City.

Lana answered the door. She was his wife, and my stepmother. She was my age. She was kind and quiet and polite and doted over my father like he was royalty.

She walked with crutches because she jumped from a seventh story balcony a few years ago and survived. She was physically cute and their relationship became a model for my future successful relationships.

We made small talk and then Dad and I left for a nearby bar.

We sat across from each other at a table away from the busy bar. We were father and son, both sitting with our long legs crossed and an arrogant posture pouring over the table. We nursed our winter beers and laughed about adulthood, because that was the most interesting topic between a father and son. The cluttered landscape of fatherhood and childhood and how the two became so poetic over some shitty Utah beer in some shitty, cold Utah winter, in the few cold breaths before your father gives up the ghost.

The snow melted. Winter left like a lion and not long after spring drifted into our hearts like a lamb.

And then I got a call from Lana.

"Your Dad didn't want me to call you. But, he's gotten pretty bad."

"Wait... What? Bad how?"

"Charles... His liver is failing. His other organs are struggling."

"He's on a transplant list though. He's at the top of the list, yea?"

Lana was quiet. Damned phones!

"Lana? Where is he on the list?"

"He pulled out of the transplant program, Charles. He's here. He's at home. He's tired of fighting."

I had taken a job selling Hondas in Escondido.

I stood on the hot lot in a shirt and tie, listening to words I hadn't prepared for. I was ten miles from the ocean but I could hear waves breaking over the jetty in Oceanside. I put my cell phone to my chest, looked into the Southern California summer sky and took a deep breath. I put the phone back to my ear.

"Can I talk to him? RIGHT NOW! Can you put him on?"

I heard rustling on the Utah end of the line.

"Hello, Son."

His voice was deep like mine. Elegant, like his had always been. But it was more humble than it had ever been. There was no power in his greeting. For the first time in my life, I couldn't hear command in his voice.

He had given up.

I put the phone back to my chest. I took a few deep breaths. I pulled a pack of cigarettes from my shirt pocket. I put the phone back to my ear and put a cigarette between my lips.

"Dad?"

I lit my cigarette with a lighter I had borrowed earlier from a fellow salesperson.

"Dad? You there?"

"Heyyyy, Son."

He was trying to be upbeat.
It was a lie. He wasn't fooling me.

"Heyyyy, Dad."

I echoed his tone.
It felt good. I meant it. I wasn't fooling. It wasn't an act for me. I wasn't hiding anything. I mean... I was trying not to cry. Beyond that, I wasn't hiding anything.

He told me he was tired. He'd been sick for nearly 25 years. Surgery after surgery. Too many medications to count. Chronic diarrhea. Constant pain. A liver transplant just meant more diarrhea and medications and hospital bills and humiliation and worry and debt.

In the weeks that followed, we spoke over the phone frequently. We talked mostly about how hard it was for his wife, Lana, and about the crystal glassware and bar set he wanted to leave me and about how his heart hurt because his daughters--my sisters, didn't want to see him or talk with him in his final hours.

Then, the call came.

"Your dad has gotten pretty bad."

"Wait. How bad?"

"He's on the couch. He seems to be relatively comfortable."

"Lana, is he awake right now? Can I talk to him for a minute?"

"He's in and out of consciousness right now, Charles. His mom and sister are here. Do you want to talk with one of them?"

NO! I DON'T want to talk with his goddamned mother or sister.

I was choking on emotion. I couldn't speak without my face and mouth trembling. My cheeks were covered in tears before I realized I was crying.

I spoke quietly and politely and carefully.

"I'd like to talk... with my Dad. Please."

Lana gave in.

"Ok. Hold on just a minute."

I hadn't prepared for this. I'd thought about it many times in recent weeks. But I hadn't given my mind fully to the idea. The idea that my father would so quickly take a turn for the worse and that we would have to say goodbye over the phone. Over the GODDAMNED phone!

In his final hours, at his most vulnerable moment, when he must have been confused and frightened, not one of his children would be there to hold his hand or to offer gratitude for holding our hands all the times we were confused and frightened.

In my Father's mortal twilight, his children would fail him. We would deny him love and comfort.

I always expected to greet the devil upon my demise. I suspect some of my sisters may be uncomfortable shaking his hand when they arrive on the other side. I'm confident we'll all have time to share a drink and ruminate. Perhaps Lucifer will inject a little morality into me and my sisters.

"Ok, Charles. I'm putting the phone to his ear. He's not really conscious, but go ahead and talk to him. Okay?"

My heart thrashed about my chest. I thought it might dash my bones and fly to the sunny coast. Away from this inland darkness. My mouth was dry and I was inhaling more than I was exhaling. Snot was running down my lip and I could see nothing but water colors.

I pulled a box of cigarettes from my shirt pocket.

My hands shook and I fumbled for one. The precise meeting of my fingertips with a slim filter seemed an impossible partnership. I finally flicked the box upward toward my mouth and caught one with my lips. I lit the cigarette and took a deep and careless drag.
Nothing mattered anymore.

There was quiet, muffled static on the other end of the line.

Then, all the world fell away. The cars that passed were muted and the planes overhead hushed their engines and the wind was still. I pressed the phone hard to my ear. And there, in the stifling summer heat, on the outside of all of my inside emotions, I could hear my father grappling for breath.

It was too much.
Oh, God.
I couldn't.
I couldn't do it.
I couldn't.

But this call was my goodbye.
This electronic connection was my hand to hold.
Surely he could hear my voice.

"Hey. Hey, Dad. Hey, Dad."

I shuddered. My ribs seemed to rend from my organs.
It was as if all of my glassy insides were shattering.
My flesh was downloading a new infrastructure and my blood was recast into ice. Thin ice. Fragile and new and hanging like mad onto a new climate.

My heart plunged like a piston. Valves forcing my sadness in and out of consciousness with so much friction, I was sure my chest would catch fire.

Our conversation was quite one-sided. I listened to his raspy breath and, at first spoke softly to him.

Soon I was yelling at him. I wanted him to tell me what he saw when he got there. If there was a God, I wanted to know about it. We had a unique relationship. I was his son. He always knew where I was and what I was doing. He could find a way to let me know. I wanted answers! Goddammit, I wanted answers.

I don't know who paid for my father's funeral.
I never asked.

I'm not even sure how to find where he's buried now.

That whole memory is like wind chimes. I can hear
something painfully soft, but I can't figure out where
the sounds are located.

They aren't actual notes.
They just feel like notes.

Soon my mother will die. I don't know who will pay
for her funeral. I won't ask anyone about that. I'll run
like so many other times, and wait for the sound of
wind chimes to fall further from my ears.

Made in the USA
Columbia, SC
16 October 2018